MW01074826

MAC BRIDGES / KENZ DURHAM

FOR WHEN I'M IN MY FEELS

A PRAYER & REFLECTIONS DEVOTIONAL

Published by Lifeway Press® • © 2022 Mac Bridges and Kenz Durham

All rights reserved. No part of this work may be reproduced or transmitted in any form or by any means, electronic or mechanical, including photocopying and recording, or by any information storage or retrieval system, except as may be expressly permitted in writing by the publisher. Requests for permission should be addressed in writing to Lifeway Press®; 200 Powell Place, Suite 100, Brentwood, TN 37027.

ISBN: 978-1-0877-6517-4
Item: 005837772

Dewey decimal classification: 152.4
Subject heading: EMOTION / DEVOTIONAL LITERATURE / WOMEN

Unless otherwise noted, all Scripture quotations are taken from the Christian Standard Bible®, Copyright © 2017 by Holman Bible Publishers. Used by permission. Christian Standard Bible® and CSB® are federally registered trademarks of Holman Bible Publishers. Scripture quotations marked (NIV) are taken from the Holy Bible, New International Version®, NIV®. Copyright © 1973, 1978, 1984, 2011 by Biblica, Inc.® Used by permission of Zondervan. All rights reserved worldwide. www.zondervan.com The "NIV" and "New International Version" are trademarks registered in the United States Patent and Trademark Office by Biblica, Inc.®

The Eight Feelings™ used courtesy of Chip Dodd and Sage Hill Counseling.

To order additional copies of this resource, write Lifeway Resources Customer Service; 200 Powell Place, Suite 100, Brentwood, TN 37027; Fax order to 615.251.5933; call toll-free 800.458.2772; email orderentry@lifeway.com; or order online at lifeway.com.

Printed in the United States of America.

Lifeway Girls
Lifeway Resources
200 Powell Place, Suite 100
Brentwood, TN 37027

Table of Contents

ABOUT THE AUTHORS

Kenz   Mac

Hiiiii, we're Mac and Kenz, the voices behind this book. We are best friends, kingdom dreamers, and probably a lot like you. We are so honored to be the ones taking you on this journey all about your feelings. Throughout this book, we will be sharing personal stories and diving into Scripture with you.

Mac Bridges is an ex-country singer from a small town in North Carolina. You probably have the wrong impression of her already because she dresses more like Beyoncé and you'll never catch her with a guitar. On the real tho, she's an incredible speaker and leader. She will fire truth at you even when you aren't ready to hear it. She's confident, strong-willed (8 on the Enneagram), and loyal. Just picture a golden retriever, pit bull mutt and you've got Mac!

Kenz Durham is everybody's best friend, ultimate hype girl, and prayer warrior. If you ever meet her, be sure to ask her to show you her speed walk—it's very impressive. Even though she's not a touchy-feely hugger, she always makes sure that everyone in the room feels included and seen. Don't be surprised by her savvy business skills and her ability to bring the house down with a fire prayer. She's a textbook 7 on the Enneagram and is sure to bring a good time no matter where she goes.

WE ARE SO GLAD YOU'RE HERE!

Have you ever found yourself in your feels?

Like woah, today I am feeling _____. Am I ever going to stop feeling this way? Or is this how I define myself now? Does God even care about my feelings?

Friend, you've come to the right place. This devotional is a place for you to come as you are to feel all the things, then encounter more of Jesus's love, grace, and goodness in light of what you're feeling.

Feelings were never meant to be ignored, suppressed, or pushed aside. You don't have to be ashamed of them! Every core feeling—hurt, lonely, sad, anger, fear, shame, guilt, and joy—have been created by God as an invitation for you to know Him deeper.

That means no matter what you're feeling at this very moment, He can handle it and wants you to bring it to Him. Because even when you don't feel it, God is doing an important work in your life.

So let's get in our feels together, so that we might encounter the beautiful richness of His loving kindness.

HOW TO USE

This devotional contains forty days of content, divided into sections based on eight core emotions. You can complete the devotions in order or out of order based on where you find yourself in your feels. There might even be days when you find yourself going back to ones you've already completed. That's totally okay, too! No matter what day you choose to do, you will always find the same three elements: Scripture, Devotion, and Prayer.

SCRIPTURE

Here's your chance to get in God's Word and let His truth speak to whatever feeling you are learning about or dealing with that day. We will always encourage you to take it a step further by opening up God's Word for yourself and reading the verse inside the context of the chapter (or if you're feeling extra motivated, the entire book of the Bible).

DEVOTION

In each devotion, you will see our real-life examples and stories tied to the truth found in Scripture to help encourage you and embrace whatever feeling you find yourself facing that day.

PRAYER

There are three prompts at the end of each day to fix your eyes on your heavenly Father, to posture your heart before Him in prayer, and to give you a safe space to cry out to Him with your honest feelings. This is the part where you truly begin to live out the truth you learned that day.

SECTION 1
HURT

Hurt is the lump in your throat, the ache in your chest, or the tears glossing over your eyes. It's the admission that something or someone has left you in pain. We all experience it differently, but if we look deep enough, it's woven throughout Scripture and through all of our stories and experiences.

Maybe it was a relationship that ended abruptly, a friend who seemed to move on without you, an invite to that spring break trip you didn't get, a parent that abandoned you, or the feeling you can vividly remember when you overheard someone saying something about you that cut deeply.

Perhaps in this moment, all of those hurtful memories from your past that you've done such a good job of tucking away, pushing aside, or looking to the bright side of are all starting to bubble to the surface. You might be tempted to close this book and never pick it up again. (Ahh, please don't do that! Hang with us.) Can we challenge you to stay, to bravely keep reading, and to be more honest with your hurt than ever before?

Remember that saying from your childhood, "Sticks and stones may break my bones, but words can never hurt me"? Can we all agree that this is a lie? Words hurt. Rejection hurts. Breakups hurt. Criticism hurts. Mean comments on the internet hurt.

So many of us have been taught to run from our hurt, cover it with a metaphorical band-aid, and simply toughen up. But just like when we ignore physical pain, our emotional pain when neglected doesn't go away, the pain only gets

worse. It starts to morph into other nasty symptoms like resentment, betrayal, and bitterness. It might even lead you to start hurting others around you as a way to cope with your own pain.

But there is good news. The beautiful thing about hurt is that when we are willing to admit it and bring it before the Lord, He invites us into the most beautiful thing— healing. He's the BEST doctor for our hurting hearts! His medicine is peace, hope, trust, reconciliation, and joy.

When we drink deeply of the gifts that only He can offer in our hurt, we can begin to heal.

God is your healer—Jehovah Rapha. He can do for you in your pain what you cannot do for yourself. You don't have to ignore the hurt that you're currently feeling. You don't have to tie it up with a pretty bow. You don't even have to dry your tears. You simply have to take that hurt to the safety of God's presence and reach out your hands to be healed in His loving arms.

WHEN I'M FEELING BETRAYED

Mac

> *"The evening meal was in progress, and the devil had already prompted Judas, the son of Simon Iscariot, to betray Jesus. Jesus knew that the Father had put all things under his power, and that he had come from God and was returning to God; so he got up from the meal, took off his outer clothing, and wrapped a towel around his waist. After that, he poured water into a basin and began to wash his disciples' feet, drying them with the towel that was wrapped around him."*
>
> *John 13:2-5, NIV*

The truth is that betrayal hurts. It's one of those feelings that leaves you second guessing everything, questioning everyone, and running for the hills to make sure that no one can ever hurt you again. Maybe it was a friend who said something horrible behind your back, a family member who didn't show up for you, or someone you loved that chose somebody else over you.

Have you ever thought about the fact that our Jesus knew what it was like to feel betrayal? Judas, one of the twelve disciples that Jesus chose to walk more closely to Him than anyone on earth, was the very person that handed Him over to the authorities to be crucified in exchange for thirty pieces of silver. This was the ultimate betrayal. The life of Jesus in exchange for some pocket change.

John 13 depicts the happenings that took place right before Jesus's betrayal. Jesus was gathered with His disciples in an upper room within the city gates of Jerusalem. We find out that Jesus knew Judas was going to betray him, but what does He do in response? Jesus gets on His knees, kneels before Judas, and washes his feet.

Have you ever thought about how powerful it is that the very night of Judas's betrayal is the very night that Jesus took on the most humble posture possible through the washing of His betrayer's feet. Jesus could have skipped over Judas. Jesus could have waited until Judas left; instead, Jesus showed the ultimate display of love in the face of the ultimate betrayal.

In verse 3, we see the "why" behind Jesus's choice. Jesus didn't lower Himself into a posture of humility from a place of weakness, but rather from a position of all authority and confidence in His Father. It was His confidence in the love of the Father that led Jesus to this beautiful display of authentic love despite the feeling of deep betrayal.

Jesus in His humanity wasn't immune to the feelings of hurt and pain that came as a result of the betrayal of somebody close. He knows what it's like to feel betrayed, so we can trust Him in our own feelings of betrayal. Because of this trust, let's be like Jesus, who in the face of our deepest betrayals, looks to our Father's acceptance. Let that assurance lead us into a Jesus kind of love where we can find healing even from our deepest feelings of hurt and betrayal.

Spend some time talking to God about any feelings of betrayal you've been experiencing.

Meditate on the heart of Jesus shown in John 13:2-5 to exhibit love to the very person who was to betray Him.

Ask for the Father's love and acceptance to be poured out in your heart in the midst of your feelings of betrayal.

WHEN I'M FEELING RESENTFUL

Mac

> *"Let all bitterness, anger and wrath, shouting and slander be removed from you, along with all malice. And be kind and compassionate to one another, forgiving one another, just as God also forgave you in Christ."*
> Ephesians 4:31-32

For nearly two years, I couldn't get this one conversation out of my head that I had with my best friend. Even though we had mended the friendship and I had forgiven her face-to-face, in the quietness of my heart, I held it against her every chance I got.

That is called the sneaky feeling of resentment.

Resentment is one of those emotions that can quietly slip under the radar while slowly but surely poisoning your heart. There are probably things from each of our pasts that we've tried to sweep under the rug, act like they don't bother us, or claim that we've moved on, but internally, we just can't seem to let them go.

Our culture loves to cancel, cut toxic people out, and place boundaries around those who have hurt us. Sometimes, this is the healthiest choice, but it is often just an excuse for us to hold tightly to our feelings of resentment.

Ephesians 4 calls us to a different path—one that is countercultural and incredibly difficult to embark upon. Verse 31 straight up says to let all bitterness—a synonym for resentment—be removed from you.

Did you happen to notice that the writer Paul says *all* bitterness? Not 90 or 99 percent, or letting that one really terrible thing someone did or said that one time slip through the cracks. We are called to empty all resentment out of our hearts, minds, and mouths, and that includes any anger, wrath, shouting, slander, or malice that might go with it.

Instead, we are to replace it with kindness, compassion, and forgiveness that stems from the undeserved kindness we've received from Jesus, who went to the cross for our forgiveness and healing while we were still broken sinners.

Spoiler alert: you do not have the power to release resentment on your own. However, when you draw near to Jesus and receive His kindness, the power of the Holy Spirit will transform and compel you to extend that same forgiveness towards others.

Resentment refuses to reconcile and always places the blame somewhere else. But when we live out of the overflow of the grace and mercy we've received from Jesus, we're able to forgive others and move towards a countercultural type of healing.

Confess any resentment that has been quietly stewing in your heart.

Reflect on the undeserved kindness and forgiveness you've received in Jesus as shared in Ephesians 4:32.

Ask Jesus to lead you toward reconciliation and healing with any person or situation you've been feeling bitterness toward.

WHEN I'M FEELING BROKENHEARTED

Kenz

> *"The righteous cry out, and the LORD hears, and rescues them*
> *from all their troubles. The LORD is near the brokenhearted;*
> *he saves those crushed in spirit."*
>
> *Psalm 34:17-18*

Psalm 34 was written from a broken heart. David, the psalmist, was defeated by life's circumstances. His friends turned their backs on him, he had to leave his home out of fear for his life, he was exhausted, and the journey had been long. He wrote this Psalm while in a literal cave with a bunch of other desperate men.

I'm sure there is a part of you that can relate to David right now. Maybe you aren't in a cave and maybe you haven't lost complete hope, but there's a good chance you feel flat-out broken—like your heart is in a million little pieces on the floor and you don't know how to put them all back together again.

Oftentimes, when we have a broken heart, we think that God is far away or like He might have walked away from us. But that's not true at all. As this Psalm declares, it's in our brokenness that He is most near to us. It's when we are weak that He is strong (2 Cor. 12:9).

God shows up right in the middle of the mess. He is our light in the darkness. He gets down low with us, holds us in His arms, and guess what? He will never leave us. There's not a moment in time when He will change His mind, walk away, or love you any less. He is always there and will never leave.

As David and these men were sitting in complete darkness together, they began to sing these words in the Psalm over themselves and their circumstances. I can imagine their eyes got a little brighter as they sang, and despite the darkness of the room, their spirits felt light again. But more than anything, I imagine Jesus being so present with them just as He is with you in your brokenness right now. And guess what? His loving presence is the best place to be.

So will you look up and cry out to Him? Will you acknowledge His presence in the room? Will you let Him embrace you in your brokenness?

Take a few moments to picture Jesus sitting beside you in your brokenness, then begin to let Him hold you and every little piece of your broken heart.

Read the Scripture from today over your brokenness and let the hope of these words renew your spirit.

Allow the Lord to simply sit there and hold you. There's no agenda, nowhere you have to be, simply experience the beauty of His presence and His embrace.

WHEN I'M FEELING REJECTED

Kenz

"For I know the plans I have for you"—this is the Lord's declaration—
"plans for your well-being, not for disaster, to give you a future
and a hope. You will call to me and come and pray to me,
and I will listen to you. You will seek me and find me when you
search for me with all your heart."

Jeremiah 29:11-13

What is your first response when you experience rejection? Ninety-nine out of a hundred would probably say that we run away. It's in the midst of rejection that you start to build walls in your heart in an attempt to not get hurt.

It's the moment you block that person on your phone. The moment you rip up that letter and throw it in the trash. It's the moment you indulge in your favorite dessert, hibernate at home, and numb the sting with the latest Netflix series.

Rejection is just plain awful. It hurts and we want nothing to do with it! But God extends us an invitation in our rejection. Do you see it there in the Scripture?

Yes, He promised the Israelites plans for "well-being, not for disaster," but there are some stronger promises in the verses that follow that we can cling to today.

"I will listen." "You will find me. "

What we don't see is anything about running away from God or hiding in the darkness. It's the opposite.

"Call to me." "Come." "Pray to me." "Seek me."

When we are faced with rejection, our first response should be to turn toward God and surrender every piece of our heart to Him. Because while we will always be at risk of receiving some form of rejection from another human, God will never reject us.

He won't turn His back on you when you call out or seek Him. He will always be there, and you can find Him anytime with open arms.

Don't run away from the One who will never turn His back on you or change His mind about you. It's okay if you don't believe that He has plans full of hope and well-being for your future. He can handle your doubts, your questions, and your hurt. Not only can He handle it, but He wants you to bring it all to Him.

Surrender your rejection to the Lord today. Let Him have all of your hurt, then wait for Him to respond. He is here for you, and guess what?

He is never leaving!

Talk to God about the rejection you've experienced recently or past rejection that you've run away from.

Meditate on the truths found in this Scripture and how it might bring you hope.

Lean into the arms of the Father, ask Him the hard questions, and listen for His voice.

WHEN I'M FEELING OFFENDED

Kenz

"You have heard that it was said, An eye for an eye and a tooth
for a tooth. But I tell you, don't resist an evildoer. On the contrary,
if anyone slaps you on your right cheek, turn the other to him also.
As for the one who wants to sue you and take away your shirt,
let him have your coat as well. And if anyone forces you to go one mile,
go with him two. Give to the one who asks you, and don't turn away
from the one who wants to borrow from you.

Matthew 5: 38-42

I have a love-hate relationship with this passage of Scripture. I mean, if you know Jesus, you know He's kind of a straight shooter and will never give you a fluffy, feel-good kind of answer. But this one, well, this just hits home.

Offense takes on a few different forms. It's the friend that didn't show up for you when you needed her the most. It's the moment your mom criticized the decision you made or the way you acted. It's the guy that commented on your weight in a season when you were already struggling to see the beauty in yourself. It's the invite you didn't get, so you're left at home alone on a Friday night.

Offense hurts!

And when we are offended, everything in us wants to crumble inside. But once we crumble, we just get mad, right? We want justice—to make those who hurt us feel what we feel, because we've convinced ourselves it's the only way we'll feel better.

But Jesus tells us to love those who offend us. To look past the offense and seek forgiveness. That's kind of a hard truth to swallow, huh?

But Jesus is empowering us in this truth to step into sacrificial love—a love that makes no sense, a love that's undeserved, a love that has no strings attached, a love like our Father's love!

All throughout His life, people rejected Jesus, didn't believe in Him, and made false accusations against Him. He was made fun of, left out, uninvited, and dismissed by even His closest friends. But at the end of His life, Jesus did something that made no sense. He died and gave His own life for the very people that spit on Him and crucified Him.

Jesus is calling each of us to that same kind of "this doesn't make any sense" love. But when we choose to love someone who has offended us, even when it feels like the most illogical decision, we are beginning to understand more of the gospel and Jesus's love that was poured out for us.

Talk to the Lord about the offense you are experiencing. Be honest with Him. Be mad with Him. He can take it all and is a safe place to be.

Reflect on this Scripture and how God might be calling you into sacrificial love. What stands out to you the most?

Ask the Lord for the words and courage to approach this person or situation with a sacrificial love.

SECTION 2
LONELY

Although there are millions of people in the world, potential "plans" to be had any night of the week, and people you can "connect" with through a couple taps on your phone, we're all too familiar with the feeling of loneliness.

Loneliness is the lack of authentic connection and a longing inside you to feel seen and loved.

We've all experienced this in some shape or form. Maybe you currently experience loneliness when it comes to your friendships—you have a ton of people you could call, but none of them really know you. Or maybe you just can't find "your people" in this season. You've tried all the things, shown up to all the events, but it still seems like no one cares. Maybe you experience loneliness through a

lack of a romantic relationship. You desperately want to build a life with someone, but you just cannot find the right guy.

Unfortunately, loneliness can't be calculated by adding up the number of relationships in your life. It's not just going to go away as soon as you start to fill your calendar with some more social hangs. It can't be cured with a few swipes on a dating app or a late night kiss from your crush. It's a quiet feeling that sneaks its way into even the happiest of moments until we find our belonging in Jesus.

Jesus is the only one that you'll ever feel fully understood by and who will forever be there for you when no one else is. You can feel safe, loved, and seen any time you are in His presence.

I recognize that some of you are still a little unsure of this. Maybe you've tried to go to Jesus in the past and it seems as if nothing changed. He feels just a little too distant in the clouds, because what you're actually looking for is a human to be in a relationship with. And while I can relate to that and I think that a desire for human connection is normal and what we were created to experience, I know that it won't ever satisfy you like Jesus can.

Believe it or not, He really is the most incredible friend. He never changes the way He feels about you. He will never once leave your side. He's alway forgiving, gives the best advice, and will be there for you when you need Him the most.

As you lean into this week and process your feelings of loneliness with Jesus, our prayer is that your friendship with Him is rekindled. As you do this, open yourself up to Him, get really honest, dig a little deeper, and wait for Him to show up. We can promise you, He will!

WHEN I'M FEELING LEFT OUT

Kenz

_____

Blessed are you when people hate you, when they exclude you, insult you,
and slander your name as evil because of the Son of Man.
"Rejoice in that day and leap for joy. Take note—your reward is great in
heaven, for this is the way their ancestors used to treat the prophets."

Luke 6:22-23

Luke 6:22-33 is a part of what is known as the Sermon on the Mount. It was one of the first messages Jesus ever spoke to His disciples, as well as to some surrounding onlookers. This sermon had four main values in becoming a true follower of Christ. His final value was what you just read in verses 22-23.

If you know a little bit about sermon writing, you'd know that the final point is often the most important. It's the thing you really want to be remembered and taken seriously. If that was the case for Jesus's sermon, we have to know that kindness and inclusivity were extremely important to Him.

I don't know who has mistreated or overlooked you, but my prayer is that you will know that Jesus sees and cares for you right now. He's frustrated with the way others have treated you and is advocating on your behalf. Not only that, but He sympathizes with you. He knows what it's like to not get the invitation and to be left on the outside.

So what does He empower us to do when we are left out or mistreated?

He tells us to rejoice and leap for joy because He has plans to show up for you, to bless you, and to reward you for withstanding bitterness from others. Because if we don't rejoice, our sinful nature will only lead us to start "sulking" in our feelings. Even though I'm certain we've all been there before, the problem with sulking is that we allow the actions of others to affect our identity.

I know it might feel nearly impossible to rejoice right now, but turn to Christ and learn from His response to being excluded. Rejoicing might look like choosing to smile when you don't feel like it or shaking off the hateful words of others. Or maybe you need to plan time to spend with Jesus. Take time to open your Bible and learn how the prophets in the Old Testament were treated to put your situation into perspective. Or maybe it's time for you to love someone else who has been left out or excluded.

The choice is yours, but my hope is that you will find reason to rejoice in Jesus today as you remember He is with you!

Confess any bitterness toward others that you've been "sulking" in the last few days or weeks.

Reflect on Luke 6:22-23 and how it empowers you to step into joy beyond your circumstances.

Ask for Jesus to reveal something to you that you can rejoice in today!

WHEN I'M FEELING UNSEEN

Kenz

———

"He heals the brokenhearted and bandages their wounds. He counts the number of the stars; he gives names to all of them."

Psalm 147:3-4

This is our God. This is your God. He's a God that cares about the big picture, the nations, the whole world, but more importantly, He cares for you, just you.

I was really sick a few months ago. Every day I woke up not feeling myself. It was hard to get out of bed and go about my normal routines. Eventually, I realized my body wasn't going to just kick the "bug" out on its own and I needed to see a doctor. I desperately picked up the phone to schedule an appointment only to find out that they were booked for two more months. I remember hanging up and feeling so defeated. I had to face the reality that I was going to have to endure this unknown illness for so much longer. It felt like no one cared and I was completely overlooked.

Some of you feel like God's booked too. Maybe it's not a belief issue for you. Like a doctor, you know He has the solutions, but it's just that He's got other important people and places to be. You feel He's probably way too preoccupied with the rest of the world's problems, the orphans, widows, poor, homeless, and so you are the least of His worries.

Let me tell you right now that that's simply a lie. Your God cares!

Just as God shows up for the nations and shows up to name every star in heaven, He shows up for you. He actually can be in a million different places at once and knows every little, big, hidden, and quiet thing in your heart and mind. I love this reminder from Psalm 139 about God's presence:

> *Where can I go to escape your Spirit? Where can I flee from your presence? If I go up to heaven, you are there; if I make my bed in Sheol, you are there. If I fly on the wings of the dawn and settle down on the western horizon, even there your hand will lead me; your right hand will hold on to me. If I say, "Surely the darkness will hide me, and the light around me will be night"—even the darkness is not dark to you.*

> *Psalm 139:7-12*

When no one else is there, God always will be. You can't escape or hide from Him. He's better than a best friend. God is more loving than your greatest love. He's more understanding than the world's best therapist. There is no better place to go than to the arms of your Father. Just as verse 10 says, "your right hand will hold onto me." He is holding onto you right now. You are never alone.

Be honest with the Lord and how you feel overlooked by Him or other people right now.

Reflect on Psalm 147:3-4 and how it helps you feel seen.

Ask Jesus to be near to you today so that everywhere you go you can feel His presence.

WHEN I'M FEELING LIKE I DON'T BELONG

Kenz

———

> *For I am persuaded that neither death nor life, nor angels nor rulers,*
> *nor things present nor things to come, nor powers, nor height nor depth,*
> *nor any other created thing will be able to separate us from the love of*
> *God that is in Christ Jesus our Lord.*
>
> Romans 8:38-39

You always have a place in the kingdom of God.

No matter your ethnicity, personality, career, past, or mistakes, you belong to the family of Christ and nothing's ever going to change that. It's a supernatural love, a love that doesn't make sense, and a love that cannot be measured or matched.

I don't know who is telling or treating you otherwise, but you have permission to stand firm in the knowledge that nothing can separate you from the love of Jesus.

Later in Romans 12:2, Paul also writes, "Do not be conformed to this age, but be transformed by the renewing of your mind, so that you may discern what is the good, pleasing, and perfect will of God."

The truth is that we were never supposed to belong to the world—our time on earth is temporary and our home is in heaven. So while we are here, the love of Christ that we see in Romans 8 should compel us to be different and live transformed.

Because when we feel like we don't belong, we often try to change ourselves in order to fit in. Have you ever been there before?

I don't know about you, but I sure have. Sometimes, it looks like slightly twisting the way I talk, changing the way I dress, spending time doing things that I am truthfully kind of over, or even compromising what I believe. Because on my loneliest days, I begin to believe that's my only option.

But what if we change what we believe when we feel like we don't belong? What if instead of believing the lies that we have to change or act differently to fit in, we cling to the truth that we belong to Him and nothing can stop that. How would that belief change the way you live and respond?

Some of you may need to get up out of your loneliness and display this kind of love toward others instead of waiting for it to come to you. Maybe it's time for you to go to the people or places that have excluded you and find restoration and healing. Some of you need to put in the work to reestablish community in your life. But as you continue to battle with loneliness and find your place of belonging, always remember that there is nothing that can separate you from the love of our Jesus. You are His forever!

Be honest with Jesus and share the pieces of yourself that maybe feel out of place or unlovable.

Meditate on Romans 8:38-39 and the weightiness of God's love for you. Let this truth penetrate any loneliness you're experiencing.

Ask Jesus for a first step in sharing this love with someone in your community or family.

WHEN I'M FEELING ON MY OWN

Kenz

_____

After dismissing the crowds, he went up on the mountain by himself to
pray. Well into the night, he was there alone.

Matthew 14:23

Have you ever imagined how lonely Jesus must have felt for most of His life?

Sure, He had all twelve of His disciples, who were some of His closest friends. Of course, He was known and recognized almost everywhere He went. He might have had people to visit and things to do, but even amongst all the people and commotion, His mission was lonely. He had a calling upon His life that no one completely understood and He carried the weight of this every single day.

I'm sure you can relate to Jesus in a similar way. Maybe you have people around you, a great family and friends, but you honestly don't feel understood. It could be somewhere God is leading you and no one totally sees why you're going in that direction. It could be something that changed about you or something you're internally dealing with but simply can't figure out how to share with anyone.

As you skim through the Gospels, you can quickly pick up on where Jesus went and what He did when He felt most on His own in His calling.

In places like Luke 5–6 and Mark 6, we see one consistent place Jesus would always go—to meet with His Father.

When Jesus started to feel the pressure of the world around Him and would grow weary, He would escape from the crowds, hit pause on His other plans with all the people that needed Him, and would even separate Himself from His own disciples. All of this to simply sit with His Father.

Jesus knew He was never really on His own. I'm sure people wondered why He spent so much time alone in the desert. I'm sure they pitied Him or made fun of Him, but I also know Jesus probably felt more seen and understood than any of them. Everywhere He went and on some of His most challenging journeys, Jesus knew He was right next to His Father.

You have this same access. On your longest days and your most challenging missions, you can meet with your Father and He will show up. He's your biggest cheerleader and the one that understands you better than your best friend. This week you might need to be like Jesus and escape the crowds, clear your schedule, and just be with Him. I cannot help but wonder what words, encouragement, and restoration you will find as you spend time with Him.

Talk to Jesus about the loneliness you've been experiencing lately and how that has affected your identity.

Read today's Scripture again and reflect on the loneliness that Jesus himself experienced through His mission on earth.

Spend a few more minutes simply being alone with Jesus. Try not to look at the clock and count down the minutes, be present with Him just as you would a friend.

WHEN I'M FEELING DISCONNECTED

Kenz

"Truly I tell you, anything you ask the Father in my name, he will give you. Until now you have asked for nothing in my name. Ask and you will receive, so that your joy may be complete."

John 16:23-24

Previously in John 16, Jesus was sharing with His disciples that there was going to come a day when He would be taken into heaven and they would no longer be able to see and feel Him in flesh.

As you can imagine, the disciples were probably freaking out a little bit. "What will that mean for us? Are You still going to feel real? Are we just going to be shouting to the clouds? How are we going to know if You are really hearing us?"

I don't know about you, but sometimes I have those same questions. It's scary how easy it is to start to feel disconnected from Jesus. It's like a friend who moves out of state, and after a couple of months go by, you feel like you've lost so much of your connection. Video calls and texts are nothing compared to cooking in the kitchen and grabbing coffee together.

Maybe you feel like that with Jesus right now. You don't know how you got here, but you simply feel like He's far away. Maybe you feel like a different person on a totally different mission, and you're not even sure how to get back to the way it once was.

Well, Jesus was prepared for this moment. In John 16, Jesus explained to the disciples that when He was gone things were going to feel different and they were going to have to ask for Him when they needed Him. What's the key word there? Ask! Jesus was teaching His disciples how to pray and call on Him because they hadn't had to do this yet.

If you are you feeling disconnected from Jesus, have you asked Him to show up in your life? Or have you been assuming He would just magically appear or speak to you when you needed Him the most?

As believers, we have unlimited, undeniable access to Jesus. But that means we have to pursue a relationship with Him just as He is pursuing a relationship with us. You have to meet with Him, you have to talk to Him, and you have to look up at Him in order to hear and see Him.

And just like when you have friendships that lose their connection, you have to remember that relationships are a two-way street. It takes honest, authentic conversation and not being afraid to ask for things that might feel intimidating.

So if you've been feeling disconnected from Jesus, ask and invite Him to show up where you need Him the most.

Open up your time with Jesus by acknowledging any wrong assumptions you've made about why you lost your connection with Him. Apologize for the ways you haven't been seeking Him.

Reflect on this moment in John 16 and how it sheds light on your situation.

Be vulnerable and ask Jesus to show up where you need Him the most today.

SECTION 3

SAD

We're all familiar with the feeling of sadness. It's what you're left with when somebody you chose to love chooses to walk away. It comes rushing in alongside disappointment when the thing you worked so hard for doesn't come to pass. It's there in the eerie silence when the person you counted on to be there tomorrow suddenly passes away.

We've all faced loss in our lives— loss of friends, family, hopes, dreams, homes, jobs, opportunities, comfort zones, confidence. The list could go on and on. Maybe the thing you've lost most recently is right there weighing on your heart like a ton of bricks. No matter how hard you've tried, you've been unable to go a single day without letting it steal today's joy from you.

Our culture often tells us that you're only allowed to be sad for a very short amount of time, then you need to get over it.

Sure, you can eat ice cream after a boy breaks up with you, but within a week's time, you should be on your "revenge body" grind. When you get rejected from the leadership opportunity on campus, you can call your mom to cry, but tomorrow you better be looking for the next best thing. When you lose someone you love, you're allowed to spend a few days mourning, but then life has to go back to normal.

Our world doesn't leave much room for feelings of sadness to exist. So oftentimes, we hide it. We stuff it down and only let it show in the tears we cry isolated and alone

at night. We start to believe that our feelings of sadness are a sign of weakness that we should be embarrassed of, that we shouldn't bother other people with, and that we should quietly wipe away our tears and keep moving.

However, when we do this, those feelings of loss can morph into self-pity. Instead of processing our pain in healthy ways, we expect others to feel what we refuse to feel. We grow bitter, irritable, critical, and cold. The sadness doesn't go away, it just evolves.

But while the world tells us to move on from our sadness, Jesus calls us to embrace it. First, to embrace Him, to run to Him, to fall at His feet, and to cast our worries, cares, and tears right there. Then, He invites us to embrace what we're feeling with Him.

Sadness isn't something to be ashamed of; rather, it's the emotion that speaks to how deeply we value something in our life—someone we love or something we've lost. The more we value something or someone, the more sadness we will feel when it's gone.

Sadness is a gift from God that helps us to show honor, recognition, and value for the things that truly matter.

WHEN I'M FEELING DISAPPOINTED

Mac

Trust in the LORD with all your heart, and do not rely on your own understanding; in all your ways know him, and he will make your paths straight.

Proverbs 3:5-6

If you grew up in church, you are probably familiar with the words of Proverbs 3:5-6. It might be one of the Bible verses you can repeat in your sleep, one you remember hearing at a Vacation Bible School, or even a verse written in pretty script on a pastel background that your mom displayed in your living room.

But let's be honest, trust in the real world looks a little bit different. True trust often only comes into the picture when things get tough. How do we trust God when our pastel world turns bleak and disappointment steps into the forefront?

I love this Proverb because it's battle tested instructions for when we face some of life's toughest seasons.

Perhaps you've felt the crushing weight of disappointment in your life recently. Maybe you didn't get the opportunity you wanted, the date didn't go well, you didn't get the grade you were hoping for, or what you thought would come to pass in this season has yet to come into the picture.

Disappointment often comes from little unmet expectations. We think things will turn out one way, then they don't, and we find ourselves upset that what we hoped for didn't come to pass.

Solomon, the wise writer of this Scripture, encourages us to release expectations and replace them with anticipation of something else. Instead of relying on our own way of thinking, processing, reflecting, and measuring success, we're encouraged to put our efforts into knowing God—His faithfulness, His character, and His sovereignty.

Our understanding of what's best for us pales in comparison to God's way of understanding what we need. When disappointment comes knocking, we can choose to either sulk in our unmet expectations or we can turn to God and get our hopes up in what He must be doing instead.

The pain of disappointment is so real, and I don't want to discount it, but I can guarantee that the goodness of our God is bigger. As you wrestle through this season of wishing for something different, ask God to change your understanding and give you a kingdom mindset for how He might be moving despite any heavy circumstances you're facing.

There's nobody better to trust with your heart, your expectations, and your next steps. Would you draw near to Him in your disappointment?

Spend some time talking to God about any feelings of disappointment you've been experiencing.

Meditate on Proverbs 3:5-6 and let it speak hope and encouragement into your feelings of disappointment.

Ask God to reveal ways you've been relying on your own understanding instead of trusting Him wholeheartedly. Lay those down before Him and ask for a renewed sense of trust.

WHEN I'M FEELING HEAVYHEARTED

Mac

___

Therefore we do not lose heart. Though outwardly we are wasting away, yet inwardly we are being renewed day by day. For our light and momentary troubles are achieving for us an eternal glory that far outweighs them all. So we fix our eyes not on what is seen, but on what is unseen, since what is seen is temporary, but what is unseen is eternal.

2 Corinthians 4:16-18, NIV

I know the feeling of a heavy heart. Don't we all? The sadness you feel inside haunts every moment no matter how hard you try to distract yourself from the pain. There are little reminders everywhere you go. It's in the produce aisle of the grocery store, at your favorite study spot, and even when you hang out with your friends.

We live in a world that can easily weigh down our hearts. It's riddled with pain, corruption, injustice, heartache, and betrayal at every corner. All it takes is a couple swipes through social media to see and feel the hurt in every part of our society. Our hearts are heavy, our souls are tired, and our shoulders are weak from the burdens we've been carrying alone.

What's that thing that has been weighing down your heart, causing you to slump your shoulders and lock your eyes on your feet?

In 2 Corinthians, the writer, Paul, was all too familiar with a heavy heart. He had been imprisoned, beaten, stoned, chased out, and rejected more times than he could probably even recall. Yet despite his own experiences, his encouragement to the church in Corinth was to not lose heart.

When our hearts hurt, we might be tempted to shut off our emotions, numb the pain, and find some way of escaping. But God calls us to not lose heart. So how do we do that?

Verse 18 says, "So we fix our eyes not on what is seen, but on what is unseen, since what is seen is temporary, but what is unseen is eternal" (NIV).

We begin to fix our eyes on the hidden joy and cause for celebration amongst the rubble and mess of our hearts, because as followers of Jesus, we have eternal hope that goes beyond our momentary pain. This means mourning and celebration don't have to live on opposite ends of the spectrum.

Would you begin to turn your gaze toward heaven and ask for God's eyes to see the things that have burdened your heart the most in a new light? Would you simply look up and lock eyes with your God who works all things together for your good, even when you cannot see it?

Don't lose heart! Turn your gaze toward Him and surrender the burdens you've been carrying alone.

Honestly talk to God about anything that has been weighing down your heart in this season.

Spend some time reflecting on 2 Corinthians 4:16-18. Ask God to reveal some of the "unseen" things that He perhaps has been doing that you might've missed.

Mourning and celebration don't have to live on opposite ends of the spectrum. Celebrate and practice simple gratitude to God in this moment despite whatever your heart has been mourning.

WHEN I'M FEELING MISUNDERSTOOD

Mac

"You have searched me, LORD, and you know me. You know when I sit and when I rise; you perceive my thoughts from afar. You discern my going out and my lying down; you are familiar with all my ways."

Psalm 139:1-3, NIV

Just recently I found myself on the front porch of my house at 10 o'clock at night with tears streaming down my face. Meanwhile, on the back porch my very confused fiancé sat trying to figure out why I had suddenly fled the scene.

I truly cannot even remember for the life of me what triggered the argument, but what I do vividly remember is how misunderstood I felt. Although I had not communicated it well, it seemed as if he just didn't get how I was feeling, and that made me feel all sorts of feels, but mostly sad.

I desperately needed someone to get what I was feeling!

I was overwhelmed with work, tired from a season of traveling, feeling disconnected from my community, guilty for not spending time with my family, and confused as to why he couldn't just read my mind, hug me while I cried, and DoorDash a stash of candy for me pronto.

As I sat on the front porch, slightly embarrassed at my sudden outburst of tears, it was almost as if God tapped me on the shoulder, and said, "Hey Mac, I get it!"

Tyler, my amazing but very human fiancé, can't always read my mind or understand my heart, but God can. He knew how tough the past few months had been on me, and how I needed to simply sit in my grief and feel it for a moment with someone who understood.

I love Psalm 139 because it speaks of how well our God knows us. He knows our every move. He searches our hearts and finds the things we've tried to hide. God knows what we're thinking, and He predicts what we need even before we do.

Maybe you've been feeling misunderstood in this season of grief, like no one truly understands what you're going through. Will you trust that your God does? Will you invite Him in to search and know your heart more than ever before? And when you feel misunderstood by the world, will you put your hope in the fact that you are seen and more understood than even fathomable in the arms of your heavenly Father?

Share with the Lord all the ways you've been feeling misunderstood by others.

Read Psalm 139:1-3 three times through in three different Bible translations. Ask God to reveal the little ways that He understands you better than anyone.

Ask God to help you forgive and find grace for the people you've been bitter towards who have perhaps misunderstood you and what you've been feeling.

WHEN I'M FEELING HOPELESS

Mac

He gives strength to the faint and strengthens the powerless. Youths may become faint and weary, and young men stumble and fall, but those who trust in the LORD will renew their strength; they will soar on wings like eagles; they will run and not become weary, they will walk and not faint.

Isaiah 40:29-31

In high school, I went on a trip to Walt Disney World with my school choir. (You might be thinking that we sang really beautiful choral pieces in robes, but it was actually a country western choir where we wore cowgirl boots and two-stepped to Patsy Cline and Hank Williams. But that's beside the point!)

On this trip, I rode a ride in Epcot for the very first time that absolutely blew my mind. I think I convinced my friends to ride it five times in a row, despite the fact that we had to wait at least an hour to get on the ride each time.

The ride is called Soarin' Around the World. It's a flight motion simulator that makes you feel like you're literally flying through the sky. They use artificial wind and scents to make the experience feel even more lifelike. On the ride you see all sorts of incredible scenery from the most magnificent viewpoint. You even find yourself gliding over a grove of orange trees in California and suddenly you smell the scent of real oranges lingering in the breeze.

Maybe my love for this ride is why Isaiah 40:31 gives me so much hope. When we trust in the Lord no matter our circumstances, no matter our pain, and no matter our hardships, He renews our strength and allows us to soar!

Soaring on a ride at Disney World is pretty cool, but can you imagine what soaring with our God is like? This kind of soaring lasts a lot longer than three minutes—it doesn't involve artificial wind and scents, and it doesn't abruptly end when the lights come back on. It's a never ending journey through life with the Lord where He sits in the driver's seat, fuels you forward, and takes you on the most scenic of routes.

Yes, there will be moments in life when it seems like your tears will never stop, the pain will not end, and the sadness won't go away. But if we allow God to be our strength and put our hope in Him, He takes us to places that we can't even fathom from the ground floor of our life. We get to mount up on wings like eagles and see life from His perspective.

There might be days when you feel like curling up into a ball and giving up, but on those days, would you surrender to a God who wants to heal and strengthen your heart? Would you trust Him? Would you put your hope in Him? Would you surrender so that you can soar with your God?

Get honest with God about how you've been feeling hopeless in this season. How have you given up on Him?

Reflect on Isaiah 40:29-31. It might feel cheesy, but close your eyes and imagine soaring with God. What does He want to show you? Where does He take you? What hope does He want to renew in you?

Ask God to be your strength in this season of hopelessness.

WHEN I'M FEELING NO ONE CARES

Mac

"Rejoice with those who rejoice; weep with those who weep."

Romans 12:15

Oftentimes, when we are sad about something we have had to let go of, we tend to assume that nobody cares and that we are meant to carry the burden of sadness alone. I've been guilty of this an embarrassing amount of times, and even worse, guilty of being the person who makes others feel like I don't care about their pain.

Several months ago, my fiancé moved from Cincinnati, Ohio, to my small town in North Carolina so we could once and for all breakup with long distance. It was a super hard decision, one that took many months of prayer, fasting, hard conversations, and discernment. However, we eventually felt peace that it was the right next step.

Although it was so fun and exciting to finally live in the same city, I could tell that the move was hard on him. He had to leave behind his friends, family, job, community, church, and the life that he had loved for over 22 years. In choosing to step into something new with me, he was having to say goodbye to so many people and places that he loved, cherished, and valued.

At first, seeing how hard the move was on him felt super annoying to me. Was I not enough for him? Did he regret his decision? Was he always going to wish he was somewhere else?

For a season, I was a total brat and hated any time he would talk about Cincinnati, plan a trip home, or answer a call from one of his old friends. But then slowly but surely, God convicted my heart and helped me to see that Tyler was mourning the loss of something that held great value in his life. That didn't negate the joy he had of starting a new life with me. Although I couldn't feel what he felt, I could honor that sadness he was feeling by celebrating how much home meant to him.

Romans 12:15 calls us to celebrate and rejoice, while also mourning and weeping together. Sadness was never meant to be kept hidden away in the depths of our heart, but rather is something that should be shared with one another. Carrying each other's burdens and allowing others to carry ours is what Jesus has called us to. It's a beautiful picture of the gospel in action that we get the honor of taking part in.

If you've been feeling like nobody cares about the sadness you're facing, would you take the risky action of honestly sharing your burdens with a trusted friend? Your sadness wasn't meant to be tightly tucked away. You don't have to do it alone! Give them the deep honor of weeping with you through your sadness.

Reflect with the Lord about who you've been inviting to carry your burdens with you. Have you been isolating yourself or are you inviting people in?

As you think about Romans 12:15, allow God to highlight the people in your life who have been rejoicing and weeping with you that perhaps you've been missing. Praise Him for giving you those people!

Ask God to open your eyes to anyone in your life who might need someone to share in their own sadness with them.

SECTION 4

ANGER

Anger is a feeling we are all pretty familiar with, am I right? Some of us might experience it more "intensely" than others, but there's no getting around the fact that we all humbly need Jesus in our anger.

Anger is the emotion we face when the waitress breaks the news that your long awaited, mouthwatering dish is sold out and you're low key boiling inside. It's the emotion you experience when you've spent one too many days with your bestie, and you've just hit your wits' end. It's when your parents are getting under your skin and everything they do and say seems to be an annoyance. It's the social media post that feels completely out of line and goes against your entire value system.

Anger has a funny way of turning us into a version of ourselves that we don't like. We often get snippy, bitter, resentful, frustrated—a lot of which we'll be processing together this week.

But what if I told you that anger might not in itself be the problem? What if our anger is actually a gift we can use to ultimately reveal or unlock the condition and contents of our hearts? What if anger actually uncovers our true passion? What if it's a tool that can be used for the benefit of all relationships?

Most of us have been taught to believe that anger is a negative emotion and we should immediately cut it from our lives. When we experience anger, we

almost feel as if we're more likely to fall short, not show enough patience, or let others get to us.

But even Jesus, the man who never sinned, felt the fullness of anger and acted upon it. His anger revealed to the people around Him a zeal, love, and commitment to the holiness of His father's house and the protection of sacred worship between God and His people. His anger compelled Him to action and to defend and protect something He deeply valued.

Anger is one of the most vulnerable emotions that we can feel because it unearths and clarifies what our hearts have been quietly yearning for and what we ultimately care about. It's like a check engine light for our hearts and our other feelings telling us and everyone around us that something is wrong and desperately needs to be fixed.

The reality though is that a lot of us haven't figured out how to lean into this side of our anger. It's become an easy excuse to sin, hate, abandon, or cancel others rather than move us toward love. We let it get ugly real quick, consume our entire being, and build up inside us until it bursts out in a way we wish it didn't.

That's why this week we're going to go to Jesus and process all this together. Our anger shouldn't be something we are embarrassed of or toss aside. Rather, it should lead us back to the feet of Jesus to be processed through His gaze and His heart. It's with Him that we can understand the deeper story it's telling, then allow Him to help us respond in love.

WHEN I'M FEELING BITTER

Kenz

God, create a clean heart for me and renew a steadfast spirit
within me. Do not banish me from your presence or take
your Holy Spirit from me. Restore the joy of your salvation to me,
and sustain me by giving me a willing spirit.

Psalm 51:10-12

If you were honest with yourself and took a moment to stop casting blame, you would acknowledge that you know bitterness isn't good for you and it isn't a badge of honor you are proud to wear.

When bitterness takes root inside our hearts, it tends to strip away our love for others and make it about ten thousand times harder to even like someone. Bitterness makes us unhappy, which leaves us having a harder time enjoying people's presence or embracing others' differences. Bitterness makes it almost impossible to say anything kind, causing everything that comes out of our mouths to have a slightly negative twist.

You've probably created distance from some people that used to be close to you because of your bitterness. Maybe you've stopped talking to them completely, unfollowed them on social media, and practically canceled them from your life. But the truth is, you cannot stop thinking about them and the hurt they've caused. It almost haunts you everywhere you go and begins to impact other relationships in your life.

That's why you have to surrender your bitterness to Jesus. Canceling them, ignoring them, or unfollowing them might feel good in the moment, but Jesus wants to offer you more.

Psalm 51 was written by the songwriter King David after he had sinned and slept with Bathsheba. He felt like a complete mess as he basically went behind everyone's backs, lied, cheated, and then failed at covering everything up. He carried the weight of this sin for so long until it totally began to eat away at Him.

David was ready to give it all back to Jesus. He wasn't looking for a quick fix or an easy way out; he was willing to surrender his heart to God—asking God to convict him, compel him, and change him.

As we close out for today, open your Bible to Psalm 51 and read it all the way through. Highlight the verses that stand out and convict you. Ask God to create a clean heart in you, renew a steadfast spirit, invite the Holy Spirit into every little bit of it, then watch Him restore your joy and heart.

The truth is we aren't stuck in our bitterness as long as we recognize our failings, repent, and humble ourselves for the Lord to renew our spirits.

Read Psalm 51 (either just a few verses or the entire chapter) out loud as a prayer and anthem over your bitterness.

Think about what it would look like for God to tangibly remove any bitterness you've held onto and renew your spirit.

Ask the Lord for a new heart and new eyes toward this person or situation that you've been holding bitterness against.

WHEN I'M FEELING FRUSTRATED

Kenz

———

Consider it a great joy, my brothers and sisters, whenever you experience various trials, because you know that the testing of your faith produces endurance. And let endurance have its full effect, so that you may be mature and complete, lacking nothing.

James 1:2-4

Before you jump into today's devotion, take a few minutes to read the Scripture passage three more times.

Life is tough. But when relationships are hard, when something is deeply frustrating and your faith is tested, you have an invitation into joy!

James, the author, said that whenever we face trials—not if, potentially, or possibly face trials—we should consider it pure joy. That means that trials and hardship are inevitable and there's no way around it. But because of our faith, we can consider our trials pure joy because it's through our hardships that God works in our hearts.

If we stayed in our comfort zones, avoided any kind of hard conversations, and stayed frustrated forever, we would not experience the power of Christ. We wouldn't grow or mature, but rather, we'd likely stay stagnant and never experience healing in the broken areas of our lives.

Any and all frustration that you are experiencing right now is an open invitation for God to build your character and deepen your faith. It's an opportunity for you to lean on Jesus more than you are probably used to, get uncomfortable in your faith, and step into the things that feel scary. Knowing Jesus allows you to turn your frustrations upside down because you are able to know His heart for you in any difficult situation. What a strong foundation to stand on!

Remember that foundation anytime someone says something unkind to you, anytime you face disappointment or heart break. Of course, it's frustrating in the moment, but because you have hope and Jesus to talk to, you don't have to live in your frustration—you can consider it joy!

Friend, there is so much joy to be found in your frustration, because the Lord is growing something beautiful inside of you.

Put all of your frustrations on the table before God and let Him see and speak into every one of them!

Read James 1:2-4 once again, then ask the Lord how He wants to build endurance and faith out of your frustrations.

Ask Jesus to begin to give you so much joy and expectations for what's to be redeemed through your situation.

WHEN I'M FEELING DEFENSIVE

Kenz

Finally brothers and sisters, whatever is true, whatever is honorable,
whatever is just, whatever is pure, whatever is lovely,
whatever is commendable—if there is any moral excellence
and if there is anything praiseworthy—dwell on these things.

Philippians 4:8

Defense can take on a lot of different forms. Some of you are a basket case of tears when you get defensive. You've probably tried to come into the conversation firm and unemotional, but your anger overwhelms you. You just want them to understand your point and your perspective.

Some of you may go silent when you get defensive. It's like you cannot even voice a word or be in the same room as the person that you're angry with, but you definitely have a lot to say!

When I'm feeling defensive, I just get mean—like really mean, shocked by the things that come out of my month, kind of mean. My husband can tell you that defense brings out my ugliest colors, and I am not proud of it. I don't want it to always be this way.

The question we must ask is: What do we do when we're feeling defensive? How can we let this emotion turn into something fruitful instead of something divisive?

Philippians 4:8 gives us a pretty great first step and maybe even a forever solution! I think it's found in those final four words, "dwell on these things."

When you're defensive, it often means you have probably been dwelling on all the wrong things—things that aren't true, honorable, just, pure, lovely, commendable, or praiseworthy. You've probably played back what they said or did a thousand times in your mind. You've probably not been thinking the nicest of things about them. You've probably not said the kindest things behind their back.

But what if you allow your heart and mind to focus where Scripture tells you to instead of allowing your sinful ways to take over? How do you think that Jesus might shift something in you that would cause you to act graciously toward them or think differently about the situation?

When we take our eyes off the situation and onto Christ, we start to see things the way He sees them and His way will always be better. His way leads us into forgiving conversations, deeper kindness, an immense amount of grace, and love for people that its been hard to love.

Choose today to dwell on the things of Christ instead of dwelling on your frustration. My prayer is that it will lead you into healing conversations with others, but most importantly, it will simply lead you back to the feet of Jesus.

Spend some time talking to Jesus about why you feel so defensive. Don't hold any part of your anger back.

Dwell on the character of Christ: what is good, lovely, pure, noble. Fix your eyes on Him and see how it changes the way you're viewing the situation.

Ask Jesus for the courage for a healing conversation or action toward this person or situation.

WHEN I'M FEELING UNDER ATTACK

Kenz

———

But mark this: There will be terrible times in the last days.
People will be lovers of themselves, lovers of money, boastful, proud,
abusive, disobedient to their parents, ungrateful, unholy, without love,
unforgiving, slanderous, without self-control, brutal, not lovers
of the good, treacherous, rash, conceited, lovers of pleasure rather
than lovers of God— having a form of godliness but denying its power.
Have nothing to do with such people.

2 Timothy 3:1-5, NIV

We all need Jesus—like A LOT. It's probably really easy to read these verses and point fingers at everyone it reminds you of. It's probably easy to let anger boil inside of you and feel more and more bitter toward them. It's probably easy to want the retreat to your Christian bubbles and comfort zones and never come out. But what I hope this Scripture reminds you of is that we all need a whole lot of grace.

Paul, the author, wrote this part of his letter to warn Timothy that Christians were going to face some harsh criticism and not always be accepted. It was a reality check to the early church that their community wasn't always going to be complete bliss and the people around them were going to stand for very different things.

Earlier in 2 Timothy 2, Paul gave a whole message about grace. In 2 Timothy 2:1, he says, "you, therefore, my son, be strong in the grace that is in Christ Jesus."

Grace is kindness when it's not deserved. It's loving others when it's not earned. It's helping people when they haven't given us anything in return.

Gosh, that's hard and especially hard when you're feeling under attack and anger's trying to rear its ugly head. But let's remember that we are all sinners, we all have shortcomings, and none of us deserve the grace that God has given us.

The truth is that you cannot lead people to Jesus if you aren't looking like Jesus. A judgmental heart is not attractive—if anything, it's quite the opposite. So if you want to step into the ultimate calling of making disciples, then you cannot get around the fact that people are going to dismiss you, hurt you, make fun of you, and disagree with you. But you have access to this grace.

Maybe you're feeling cornered right now, maybe you feel like no one understands you or can see your point of view. Maybe people have said mean things to you and hurt you deeply. While I know this is hard and often makes no sense, I want to challenge you to step into grace. It might look like a kind response, something you can do to make them feel loved. It might be the simple words "I'm sorry," or it might be an invitation or a thoughtful gift. Ask Jesus how He might be calling you into grace and see how He moves in your life because of it.

Spend some time reflecting on the grace that Jesus has given you.

Picture Jesus standing with you as you have been under attack. How does He extend grace in the same situation?

Follow Jesus's footsteps and exemplify His grace in this relationship.

WHEN I'M FEELING RESENTFUL

Kenz

Friends, do not avenge yourselves; instead, leave room for God's wrath, because it is written, Vengeance belongs to me; I will repay, says the Lord. But If your enemy is hungry, feed him. If he is thirsty, give him something to drink. For in doing so you will be heaping fiery coals on his head.

Romans 12:19-20

This feels a little intense, right? Let's dig in a little deeper and see what it might be saying to us in our resentment.

"Friends, do not avenge yourselves" (v. 19). I did a quick search to better understand the word avenge, and I found that Merriam-Webster defines it as "to exact satisfaction for (a wrong) by punishing the wrongdoer."[1] Have you ever wanted to punish someone for something they did to you? Well, this verse is clear in saying that we shouldn't and that means we can't treat others with rude, mean, or disrespectful behavior even if it's what we experienced from them.

"Instead, leave room for God's wrath, because it is written, vengeance belongs to me; I will repay, says the Lord" (v. 19). This is a pretty intense way of saying that it's better in the Lord's hands than in yours. Even though you might be the one who was wronged, you still aren't perfect. But God and His justice are both perfect, so He will not let any wrong go unpunished. He will fight on your behalf.

"If your enemy is hungry, feed him. If he is thirsty, give him something to drink" (v. 20). As you trust in the Lord to be just, your only requirement is be the hands and feet of Jesus to others and let Him take care of the rest.

But what does it mean to be the hands and feet of Jesus? To go out of your way for others in order to show the love and kindness of Jesus even when it might be difficult for you.

"For in doing so you will be heaping fiery coals on his head" (v. 20). It is all making sense now (lol). This seemingly goofy imagery of "heaping coals on someone's head" was Paul's way of saying that we can defeat our enemies and overcome our resentment by making them our friends.

I don't know how you might be dealing with resentment, but I do know that it will always be better in God's hands than in yours. The tighter you hold onto resentment, the harder it's going to be for God to redeem the relationship. The best thing you can do today is fix your eyes on the things of Christ and start to practically serve Him in any way you can. As you do so, I believe that your mind, spirit, and perspective will all begin to change.

Invite the Lord into your resentment instead of hiding it from Him or keeping it quiet.

Open your heart and hands to surrender the relationship or situation fully back to Jesus. Try to picture what it would look like to actually hand it over to Him.

Ask the Lord how you can step into kindness and love others in the waiting.

---

1. *Merriam-Webster*, s.v. "avenge," https://www.merriam-webster.com/dictionary/avenge.

SECTION 5

FEAR

Fear comes in all different shapes and sizes. Growing up, perhaps, it was those monsters under your bed. Maybe in high school you were afraid of cliff jumping with your friends at the lake (me still). Recently, perhaps your fears have turned to navigating a new scary city all on your own or the fear of getting rejected by a guy you've been crushing on. Maybe what you've been afraid of recently feels even more serious—the health of a family member or how you're going to pay this month's bills.

We all have fears that we've probably gotten pretty good at hiding and dealing with on our own. This is how anxiety typically enters the picture. We suppress our fear or try to manage it on our own terms, so we wind up enslaved to our worries and our what ifs.

Oftentimes, especially in Christian circles, when we get up the courage to finally confront these fears out loud within our community, we're met with well-intentioned remarks and comments, such as, "Do not fear! God's got you! It's going to be okay! Don't worry about it!"

These words can feel comforting for a moment, but they don't always offer long-term relief. They are like a spiritual Band-Aid that hides your deepest fears without dealing with the pain. So what do you do in the aftermath when you're lying in bed at night and the fear is still very much alive?

The hard truth for many of us is that you can't magically pray or worship fear away. Because what if fear in itself isn't actually the problem? What if the problem is how we've been taught to manage our fears?

Psalm 111:10 says, "The fear of the LORD is the beginning of wisdom; all who follow his instructions have good insight. His praise endures forever."

While the world tells us to do whatever it takes to overcome our fears, Scripture says that fear can actually be a gift. It leads to life, contentment, protection, confidence, and ultimately God Himself!

Fear recognizes that we as human beings have limitations and are in deep need of a loving, forgiving, protecting, and saving God. It is what allows us to admit our weaknesses, cry out to God for help, and invite Him to provide for us in ways that we never could for ourselves.

So when you face unavoidable moments of fear in your life, you can try to overcome them on your own, leading you to worry, control, and anxiety. Or you can let fear lead you to embrace what you're scared of, release control, and reach out for help from your loving, heavenly Father.

WHEN I'M ANXIOUS ABOUT EVERYTHING

Mac

"When I am afraid, I put my trust in you. In God, whose word I praise— in God I trust and am not afraid. What can mere mortals do to me?

Psalm 56:3-4, NIV

Have you ever felt defined by your anxiety? Like no matter who or what you try to be, it feels as if anxiety always seems to win the day.

Maybe you tried to muster up the courage to deliver that presentation with boldness, but your knees wouldn't stop shaking and your mind wouldn't stop telling you that you were a failure.

Maybe you've been feeling anxiety about your relationship. You can't stop obsessing over whether or not he's the perfect guy for you, so you've started to pull back all together.

Perhaps you've been anxious about what comes next in life. What if you can't find a job and you're forced to move back in with your parents? Rather than applying for jobs, you've been spiraling mentally and feeling too debilitated to do anything.

Sometimes we get so comfortable and used to our anxious habits that we forget to get to the bottom of where they're coming from. We treat the symptoms rather than identifying the cause. Anxiety is almost always rooted in some sort of fear—fear of the future, fear of failure, fear of what others might think, and so on. What fear is hiding under your anxiety?

Psalm 56:3 says, "When I am afraid, I put my trust in you" (NIV). Did you notice that it doesn't say, "I *never* fear, so I put my trust in you."

It's quite the opposite actually. Fear and anxiety can actually produce trust! Scripture does not promise us a life without fear or total immunity from anxiety. Therefore, we don't have to feel ashamed about feeling anxious. Instead, we can look to Scripture for how to fight back when anxiety strikes.

When you feel fear begin to express itself as anxiety, would you take a moment to trust God? Go before the Lord and name whatever it is you're afraid of at His feet. Read His Word and look for the promises that He has made for you. Take the pressure off of your shoulders to overcome whatever it is that you fear alone and face it with Him!

First Peter 5:6-7 says, "Humble yourselves, therefore, under the mighty hand of God, so that he may exalt you at the proper time, casting all your cares on him, because he cares about you."

We are called to cast our cares and our anxieties upon the Lord. Your anxiety cannot and will not win the day when you are trusting and walking alongside your sovereign, all-powerful, and caring God.

Spend some time with the Lord identifying what the root fear is underneath your anxiety.

Read Psalm 56:3-4 several times out loud and ask God to give you supernatural trust in Him despite whatever it is that you're afraid of.

Praise God for how He has cared for you in the past and let it build faith in you for how He might provide for you in the future.

WHEN I'M AFRAID
I'M NOT ENOUGH

Mac

> But Moses replied to the LORD, "Please, Lord, I have never been
> eloquent—either in the past or recently or since you have been speaking
> to your servant—because my mouth and my tongue are sluggish."
> The LORD said to him, "Who placed a mouth on humans? Who makes a
> person mute or deaf, seeing or blind? Is it not I, the LORD? Now go!
> I will help you speak and I will teach you what to say."
>
> Exodus 4:10-12

This conversation from Exodus 4 between Moses and God makes me low-key giggle because it's oddly familiar to so many of the dialogues I have with the Lord on a daily basis. Our convos typically go something like this:

Me: God, I'm not the girl for the job! I don't know what I'm doing. I messed it up last time. I'm not good enough.

God: This isn't about you. This is about what I want to do through you.

Me: Are you sure? I'm scared! Can you pick someone else?

God: Nope, you're the girl I want to use. But I will be with you!

Okay, so I've never heard God audibly say any of these things to me directly, but it helps paint the picture of what goes on in my heart and mind. I'm always scared and obsessed with my insufficiencies when God is quick to remind me of His sufficiency.

In Exodus 4, God appeared to Moses in the form of a burning bush and commissioned him to go back to his homeland of Egypt to tell Pharaoh to set the Israelites free from slavery. Moses was terrified out of his mind, so he tried to tell God why he shouldn't be the one for the job. God quickly corrected Moses by reminding him that all things were under God's control and that He would help Moses every step of the way.

Is there something in your life right now that you feel God has called to do, but you're terrified to obey? Perhaps all you can think about is all the ways you're not enough, the ways you've messed it up, and how you will never measure up.

Can I encourage you to do it scared? Sometimes, it's in the moments when we come toe-to-toe with our biggest fears and we're overwhelmed by what we lack that we begin to see our deepest calling, our biggest passion, or our God-given purpose.

Let your fear of not being enough build faith in you so that you can trust and relinquish control to the One with all things under His control and whose power is shown even greater amongst your weaknesses, your mistakes, and your failures. Girl, do it scared because He is with you!

Confess the reasons why you haven't felt enough recently to the Lord.

As you reflect on Exodus 4:10-12, get honest with God about how like Moses you've tried to "back out" of the things He might be calling you into.

Ask God to give you a vision for what it could look like to step into your calling scared with Him.

WHEN I'M CONFUSED ABOUT WHAT TO DO

Mac

———

Therefore, I remind you to rekindle the gift of God that is in you through the laying on of my hands. For God has not given us a spirit of fear, but one of power, love, and sound judgment.

2 Timothy 1:6-7

There will be tough decisions we all have to make throughout our lives—who to be friends with, where to go to college, what to major in, where you're going to work, who you're going to marry, and so on. Even deciding what you're going to eat for lunch feels hard sometimes.

Oftentimes, the fear of making the wrong choice can overwhelm us and leave us feeling either stuck or like we have to choose the safer option.

In these verses, Paul reminded Timothy that God did not give him a spirit of fear, but one of power, love, and sound judgment. This Scripture reminds us that when we are fearful about a decision that we have to make, we are called to not discern in fear but by what God has so graciously given us access to in Him. Let's look at what that is according to 2 Timothy 1.

A spirit of power — Thank goodness that when we are making hard decisions, we aren't alone in them. We have the supernatural power of God within us! Decisions that we choose to make might not always add up to the natural world because we have a supernatural kingdom mindset. This means that with the help of His Spirit, we can choose what feels impossible or makes no sense to the world.

A spirit of love — When we have to make scary decisions, we can hold fast to the spirit of love within us. The power of God isn't like the power we know of from this world that's often represented in muscles, military might, and violence. It's the power displayed through loving, honoring, and serving one another. When discerning through a tough decision, consider whether or not your choice puts love on display.

A spirit of sound judgment — Finally Paul talks about a spirit of sound judgment. The Greek word used here implies the idea of a peaceful, calm, and centered mind that stands in the face of the utter chaos and confusion that can often come from scary choices.[1] We might be tempted to make a choice from the anxiety and panic, but God is offering us a spirit of peace that allows us to choose not necessarily what is safe, but rather what is godly and honorable to Him.

When you stand at the crossroads of a decision that feels daunting, overwhelming, and downright scary, remember that you were not given a spirit of fear. Call upon the Holy Spirit who equips you with power, love, and sound judgment.

Get super honest with the Lord about the decision you've been trying to discern and how you might be playing it safe.

As you think about 2 Timothy 1:7, ask God to show you what it looks like to act according to a spirit of power, love, and sound judgment.

Sometimes, we worship the answer more than the One who gives answers. Spend some time just worshiping the Lord and thanking Him for who He is rather than seeking answers.

1. David Guzik, "2 Timothy 1," *Enduring Word*, October 19, 2021, https://enduringword.com/bible-commentary/2-timothy-1/.

WHEN I'M SCARED OF WHAT'S TO COME

Mac

———

Then the apostles returned to Jerusalem from the hill called the Mount of Olives, a Sabbath day's walk from the city. When they arrived, they went upstairs to the room where they were staying. Those present were Peter, John, James and Andrew; Philip and Thomas, Bartholomew and Matthew; James son of Alphaeus and Simon the Zealot, and Judas son of James. They all joined together constantly in prayer, along with the women and Mary the mother of Jesus, and with his brothers.

Acts 1:12-14, NIV

In Acts 1, we find the disciples gathered together in a scary moment. Jesus had just ascended into heaven and His final instructions were to go back to Jerusalem to wait for the promised Holy Spirit to come.

Can you imagine what they must've been feeling? Jesus was their shepherd, leader, unifier, savior, and friend. He was their glue! They had been through so much emotionally in the weeks before—the arrest of Jesus, the crucifixion, His surprise resurrection, and those random sneak attack appearances—what a roller coaster!

Jesus had commissioned them with the tall task of going and making disciples of all nations, and then just like that, He was gone again! All they knew was that they were to wait in Jerusalem on the promised Holy Spirit. I'm sure they were terrified out of their minds about the possibility of persecution and how on earth they were going to do what Jesus did without Him.

Despite all this, I love what we see the disciples do in Acts 1:12-14, because it speaks so much to what we can do when we face moments of uncertainty about what lies ahead of us.

First off, they waited on the Holy Spirit. They didn't forget Jesus's instructions; they simply obeyed by returning to Jerusalem and waiting on the Spirit of God to fall upon them and be the catalyst to their next move.

Second, they joined together in community. Here we see Jesus's disciples gathered in a room and united in what Jesus asked them to do.

Third, they were constantly in prayer. As they waited for their next move, they chose to go to their knees and seek answers through the posture of prayer. (Don't you wish you could've been a fly on the wall during those sacred days before the arrival of the Holy Spirit?)

When we are afraid or unsure of what's to come, we can respond like the disciples. First, we wait on the Holy Spirit to move within us and lead us in our next step. Second, we find a Christ-centered community to walk and discern through what scary things perhaps lie ahead of us. Third, we are consistent in our posture of going before the Lord and laying our cares, concerns, requests, and praises at His feet.

Spend some time with the Lord just waiting on His Spirit. Let Him stir up courage and boldness in your heart.

Confess how you've turned to things other than prayer to try and overcome your fears on your own.

Ask God to highlight people in your world that you can join together in community with and unite around a love and trust in Jesus.

WHEN I'M FEELING INTIMIDATED

Mac
———

I love you, LORD, my strength. The LORD is my rock, my fortress, and my deliverer, my God, my rock where I seek refuge, my shield and the horn of my salvation, my stronghold. I called to the LORD, who is worthy of praise, and I was saved from my enemies.

Psalm 18:1-3

David was no stranger to intimidation. Intimidation was all around him. There were the Philistines, the giant Goliath, and King Saul, his once mentor who would stop at nothing to end David's life. It seemed that everywhere David went, people who wanted to harm him seemed to follow.

Perhaps you've felt surrounded by some type of enemy in this season. Maybe they aren't necessarily out to get you with spears, but they've used their power to create fear or intimidation in your mind. You find yourself afraid of how they might hurt you, manipulate you, or overwhelm you on a daily basis. Unfair intimidation from parents, leaders, boyfriends, bosses, professors, and so on is unfortunately very real in many of our experiences.

What's so powerful about David's story is that no matter what enemy or circumstance he faced, he remained steadfast in his dependence upon the

Lord. David knew that he couldn't change his situation, or magically get rid of the people that wanted to harm him, but he could always take cover in the goodness of his God.

This is why all throughout the psalms, David sings songs about God being his rock, his refuge, his shield, his stronghold, his covering, and his protector. When intimidation from his enemies would begin to build, David would flee to the secret place with His God. He would praise Him, worship Him, and lament about his pain and fear, and David would remind himself of the character of God.

No matter what intimidation you are facing right now, know that your God is waiting with open arms for you to seek refuge in Him. He can build a fortress of sweet protection around your heart, so that when intimidation tries to attack again, you are safe within His presence. Call upon God's name, flee to His loving embrace, and let Him be your strength in the face of your enemies.

Read all of Psalm 18. Afterward, close your eyes and imagine being closely embraced by Him.

Share with the Lord how you've been feeling intimidated in this season. How have you been trying to face it on your own?

Allow God to build strength, boldness, and courage in you. Ask Him to reveal specific ways that He has equipped you to face whatever or whoever has been intimidating you.

SECTION 6

SHAME

Have you ever convinced yourself you are unworthy of a calling? Maybe you've felt too messed up to be a recipient of someone's love? Or worse, too far gone to be loved by your heavenly Father?

That's what shame feels like. It's a voice that distorts our identity in who God has called and created us to be. Different from guilt, shame has less to do with something we actually did, but rather a lie we're believing in the way we view ourselves.

Maybe it was something your parents or siblings spoke over you at an early age, telling you that you weren't good enough and you still think about it today. Maybe it was an out of line comment from your first boyfriend that has never left your head. Maybe it was a sin from your past that's long gone now, but you still feel like a total failure. Maybe it was a dream job that you didn't get and has kept you from putting yourself out there again.

A lot of the time, we are unaware of our shame. We make decisions, meet new people, apply for jobs, and go about life totally oblivious of this quiet whisper ultimately holding us back or tearing us down. But then some of us are completely aware of our shame. It is attached to almost everything we do from the moment we wake up and look in the mirror to the time we get in bed at night.

Shame, no matter where it comes from or how big or small it might feel in your life, is detrimental to your calling and purpose here on earth. It strips you from your potential and leaves you hidden from the world.

That's why Jesus so desperately wants in! He wants to intervene, restore, and redeem every lie you believe about yourself. Our shame is an invitation into humility and to rely more deeply on our Father. It can restore your relationship with Him and so many more around you.

The truth is, He is not surprised or scared by your failures, mess ups, or past sins. He doesn't see you as impure, not enough, or too far gone. He stands ready with open arms for you to step into His invitation of grace and transformation.

My prayer is that this week you will have the courage to humble yourself before the Lord and leave all your shame at His feet.

When Jesus looks at you, He is not ashamed of you. He isn't embarrassed to call you His. He doesn't see the weight of your past. He looks at you and sees His beloved daughter for whom He is calling into a new future.

That is good news!

WHEN I'M FEELING DEFINED BY MY PAST

Kenz

———

Brothers and sisters, I do not consider myself to have taken hold of it.
But one thing I do: Forgetting what is behind and reaching forward
to what is ahead, I pursue as my goal the prize promised by
God's heavenly call in Christ Jesus.

Philippians 3:13-14

If you don't know who the writer of Philippians is, let me introduce you. His name is Paul, and well, he had one wild past! Paul (who was at first called Saul) used to persecute Christians and was on a mission to totally destroy the church. He blatantly hated people that followed God and wanted nothing to do with Him all together.

One day, Paul was traveling to Damascus when the Lord showed up and changed his life. Acts 9:3-4 says, "As (Paul) traveled and was nearing Damascus, a light from heaven suddenly flashed around him. Falling to the ground, he heard a voice saying to him, 'Saul, Saul, why are you persecuting me?'" After, Paul fell to the ground and cried out "Who are you, Lord?" (v. 5). Then, God called him on mission.

When Paul began proclaiming Jesus as the Son of God, people were shocked to say the least. They had no clue why or how God could've used someone with a messy past like Paul. I can only imagine the questions Paul asked God in those days, but I picture something like: "Don't you know what I have done, Lord?"

But the Lord had no hesitation to use Paul for His kingdom purposes. Because from the moment that Paul encountered God on the road to Damascus, he was a new creation—the past was gone, and nothing mattered except for what was ahead!

That's what the Lord thinks of you too! In 2 Corinthians 5:17, Paul writes, "Therefore, if anyone is in Christ, he is a new creation; the old has passed away, and see, the new has come!" This is the truth! You are not your past mistakes. You are not defined by what someone spoke over you. You are more than what you see in the mirror. If you are a follower of Jesus, you are a new creation and God has called you according to His glorious purposes.

Will you choose to believe that for yourself? Like Paul, will you hold tightly to the mission at hand and press on for the sake of "the prize promised by God's heavenly call in Christ Jesus" (Phil. 3:14)?

Spend some time talking to the Lord about the thing in your past that you've let hold you back.

Read all of Acts 9 for yourself and reflect on Paul's testimony and how it speaks to your story.

Ask the Lord to show you how He is inviting you into mission with Him and how He can redeem your past in order to fulfill your God-given calling.

WHEN I'M FEELING LIKE A FAILURE

Kenz

———

"You did not choose me, but I chose you. I appointed you to go and produce fruit and that your fruit should remain, so that whatever you ask the Father in my name, he will give you."

John 15:16

It's that closed door, that rejection letter, that failing test score, and that time you put yourself out there only to be completely ignored. Maybe you didn't say it out loud in the moment, but inside, you sure believed that you were a failure.

Failures often make us go inward. They take us back to our comfort zone. We get lazy and complacent, then we stop believing the truth that God chose us and has called us to go.

He chose you. He sought you out. He picked you out amongst the crowd. Have you ever thought about this? That before you chose Him, He chose you.

Sometimes we think that we have to be perfect before He can love us. Or we convince ourselves that we have to become less sinful before He can use us. But the truth is, He chose you first. Even after knowing you would fail time and time again.

One of my favorite parts of this Scripture is that after Jesus says He chose you, He continues on by saying He appointed you to go. That means Jesus didn't choose you for nothing; He is calling you to live with purpose and on mission for Him.

Instead, we often let our failures define us and convince us of the opposite: 1) No one could want us; 2) We have nothing to offer. But despite your mess-ups and failures, this truth found in John 15:16 will never change.

God will always want you and you will always have purpose.

Are you ready to get back up on your feet and start living like it? To live like He chose you—regardless of what someone else has said. To live like you have purpose regardless of if you can't see His potential in you.

Talk to the Lord about your failures and let Him into the areas you are insecure about.

Read today's verse again. Ask the Lord what truth you need to hold onto and believe about your future.

Take the first step in wherever God is calling you to go.

WHEN I'M FEELING INSECURE

Kenz

But he said to me, "My grace is sufficient for you, for my power is
perfected in weakness." Therefore, I will most gladly boast all the more
about my weaknesses, so that Christ's power may reside in me. So I
take pleasure in weaknesses, insults, hardships, persecutions, and in
difficulties, for the sake of Christ. For when I am weak, then I am strong.
2 Corinthians 12:9-11

This Scripture has been my anthem. I'm not very good at memorizing Scripture, but this one I could recite to you whenever, wherever. It has been my rock when it's felt like my identity has been deeply shaken.

I'll never forget the parent-teacher conference I had in the second grade. I sat there at the table as my teacher told my parents it'd probably be best for me to be held back another year. I wasn't sure the reason why—all I translated it to was that I wasn't smart enough or mature enough to move forward. I felt like a total failure and it was so embarrassing!

Honestly, ever since this moment, I've battled insecurities. I never felt like I measured up to my peers and it's been hard for me to believe in any of my God-given gifts. This thirty minute conversation in the second grade took a shot at my identity and it has taken me years to rebuild. That's why this passage has been my anthem. It's the truth that I have combated every lie from Satan, every negative thought, and every naive comment that someone else has made about me.

If His power is made perfect in our weaknesses, this means that He can move through us in more powerful ways when we bring our insecurities before Him. When we feel inadequate or incapable, we can remove our pride and cling to the Lord. The Scripture gives us permission to be proud of our weaknesses as it gives more room for Jesus to move in our lives.

Before I go on stage, before I speak up, before I pray out loud, even before I wrote this devotional, I bring my insecurities before the Lord. I invite Him to be a part of the process, to move through my words, and to take the front seat. Our insecurities leave room for the presence of God to move more powerfully in our lives!

So the next time an insecurity tries to creep in, lean into it a little further. Learn how to embrace the things that feel like weaknesses, then invite the Lord into them. I believe that in doing so you will stay so deeply connected to the Lord that you will see Him rebuild confidence in your spirit, and you'll begin to recognize that maybe your greatest weaknesses are actually your greatest strengths.

Identify any insecurities or weaknesses that you have been facing recently.

Read 2 Corinthians 12:9-11 out loud two or three times.

Invite the Lord into any insecure parts of your life, then watch how you become more dependent on Him.

WHEN I'M FEELING LIKE GIVING UP

Kenz

"So I said to you: Don't be terrified or afraid of them! The LORD your God who goes before you will fight for you, just as you saw him do for you in Egypt. And you saw in the wilderness how the LORD your God carried you as a man carries his son all along the way you traveled until you reached this place."

Deuteronomy 1:29-31

This Scripture was written to the Israelites in a super fearful moment. They had just spent the last forty years in the wilderness and had finally made it to the edge of the promised land—a land they had been anticipating and waiting on for years!

But moments before getting there, the Israelites heard that there were giants and that they should fear for their lives. Moses, full of passion, spoke these words in Deuteronomy over their fears. He was reminding them that the God who had fought for them in the past was going to stand right beside them in the future. Although times had been challenging, the Israelites couldn't have pointed out one instance where the Lord didn't pull through for them. He had never let them down.

Just moments before God was going to fulfill His biggest promise yet to the Israelites, Moses had to once again remind them that the Lord would fight for them and would carry them all the way through to what He had promised.

Just as Moses spoke with passion over the Israelites people, the Lord wants to speak this over you today.

Although things might be tough right now or maybe even the past few years have been challenging, the Lord hasn't left you! God never promised a life without trials and tribulations and that everything was going to be a walk in the park once you started following Him. But you can be sure of this: the Lord is right beside you in the midst of your hardship. The Lord will never leave you, He will fight for you, He will advocate on your behalf, He will be faithful to you, and He will fulfill what He has promised.

Don't give up here and miss all the promises that the Lord has ahead. Don't throw in the towel and forget how far He has already brought you! There is so much more ahead. Press on to the prize, lock eyes with your Father, and be reminded that He has always been by your side.

Spend some time reflecting on moments from your past when the Lord has been there for you. Write them down in a journal or at the bottom of this page.

Think about Deuteronomy 1:29-31 and how it reminds you of your confidence in the Lord regardless of what's ahead.

Pray and ask the Lord for an extra bit of courage and energy for this day and for the mission He has for you as you walk forward.

WHEN I'M FEELING LIKE SOMETHING IS WRONG WITH ME

Kenz

_____

For it was you who created my inward parts; you knit me together
in my mother's womb. I will praise you because I have been remarkably
and wondrously made. Your works are wondrous, and I know
this very well. My bones were not hidden from you when I was made
in secret, when I was formed in the depths of the earth.
Your eyes saw me when I was formless; all my days were written
in your book and planned before a single one of them began.

Psalm 139:13-16

Let's talk about child birthing! I have yet to birth a child, but I'm assuming it's pretty miraculous. What begins as a tiny little cell turns into a real, life-sized baby human in a matter of months. It has eyes, little limbs, a smile, a personality, it poops and pee.

LIKE WHAT?

God picked out every little thing about that baby. He made him or her exactly the way He wanted and He did it with intention. You better believe our God didn't just whip up something without any thought and just hoped for the best. Even with all of the babies born every day across the world, God knows the exact amount of hairs on their heads. He picked and placed every freckle, every curve, and every itty bitty thing about them.

This is how God created you too! Nothing about you is an accident or mistake. You were designed and created just the way He wanted you to be. That includes your personality, the way you look, the family you were given, and the way it all began.

There's not a piece or part of you that He would take back or make differently. Our God doesn't make mistakes.

As you go before the Lord today, bring those things that you've been doubting about yourself—the things you are most ashamed of, the things you wish were different about your body, and the parts of your story you aren't proud of. Let the Lord speak this truth from Psalm 139 over you. He wants to remind you of the identity you have in Him as His beautiful, unique, and special creation. Anchor your confidence in this truth.

Be raw, real, and honest with God about the parts of yourself that you might be ashamed of or simply mad about.

Reflect on Psalm 139:13-16 and the miracle of creation.

Write down what you know to be true of yourself according to this Scripture (and any other Bible verses you might know or can find). Feel free to use the space below and come back to this page every time you need to be reminded.

SECTION 7

GUILT

Guilt. It's one of those feelings that we've all probably tried to avoid at all costs throughout our lives. It's a funny feeling because as much as we try to avoid it, guilt has a peculiar way of sneaking into our hearts and minds more often than we'd perhaps care to admit.

It's the feeling you get after talking poorly of a friend. The comment just slipped out so easily and you would do anything to take it back. It's the sense of regret you get when you suddenly snap at your mom on the phone. It's the feeling you get the morning after a night out with your friends. You were just trying to have a good time and fit in, but the hangover wasn't even close to worth it. It's that thought in the back of your mind nagging you when you've gone days without opening your Bible and talking to Jesus.

A lot of us have put shame and guilt in the same category, but they're vastly different. Shame is rooted in our identity. It's the feeling that comes from lies and fallacies that we believe about who we are or who we aren't. Guilt on the other hand is associated with our actions and behavior. It's a feeling we experience when we do something that goes against our values.

The feeling of guilt is often in the aftermath of doing something that stands in the face of what God has called us to.

The result of guilt has two very distinct outcomes. The first option is we run from it, deny it, or justify our actions only to leave ourselves in a prideful mess. On the other hand, we can confess it, let God use it to refine us, accept forgiveness, and step into freedom from it.

And while we are all guilty of past sins or mistakes, we are also all met with grace because of the kindness and mercy of our God. He forgives us when we confess our sin, and not only that, He gives us the Holy Spirit to help us live differently in the aftermath of our mistakes. This is the undeserved invitation that we get from Jesus in our guilt.

When we confess our guilt to Jesus, He can allow something extraordinarily beautiful to come from it. Guilt actually helps us to draw better boundaries, teaches us how to ask for forgiveness, how to say no in the future to things that harm others, and leaves us dependent on the grace of our God, rather than our attempts at being perfect.

The next time that you feel guilty, instead of ignoring it or sweeping it under the rug, would you run to the feet of Jesus and confess whatever sin led you to this point? Your guilt could be the catalyst for beautiful stories of reconciliation, healing, forgiveness, and freedom.

WHEN I'M FEELING LIKE A TERRIBLE FRIEND

`Mac`

———

The one who conceals his sins will not prosper,
but whoever confesses and renounces them will find mercy.

Proverbs 28:13

Kenz and I have been friends for over ten years. I mean it when I say that we have been through some super high highs and some extremely low lows. Our friendship has withstood major life changes, running a ministry together, writing books together, making hard decisions that deeply affected one another, and countless moments when we didn't see eye-to-eye.

One of our toughest seasons of friendship was a few years out of college in the midst of a six-month long argument. There are many details to the story, but essentially we didn't agree about something, and in the process of our disagreement, we each did and said a lot of hurtful things.

I'll never forget one day when Kenz asked me to go for a walk. As we walked the streets close to our office that we had meandered countless times before, she began to super honestly confess so many things that she regretted from the months before. It was the most sincere apology I had ever received. It wasn't just a quick "sorry" so we could move on. It was thorough, it was detailed, and it was even brutally honest at times.

As Kenz shared her heart with me on that walk, all of the feelings of anger, bitterness, and resentment that I had clung tightly to for the past six months began to melt. All I wanted to do was forgive Kenz and confess all the ways in which I had wronged her too.

That's the power of confession that Proverbs 28:13 speaks of. When we do the hard work of confessing our sin to God and the people we have hurt, it sets up the most beautiful moments of forgiveness and reconciliation. I had done just as many hurtful things to Kenz as she had done to me. She had every right to hold onto bitterness forever and use it as an excuse to avoid her own guilt. Praise God that instead she let her guilt lead her to lay her pride aside and admit what she had done wrong, thus bringing healing to our friendship.

Perhaps you've been feeling guilty about something in one of your friendships or relationships—something you said, something you did, or something you failed to do. Maybe you've been justifying that guilt with a million reasons why your friend doesn't deserve an apology or reconciliation.

Would you do the hard thing of laying your pride aside and being the first to confess your mistakes even if that friend seems undeserving? The ownership of your part could be the catalyst for God-centered healing and forgiveness in your friendship. Don't run from your guilt. Take it to Jesus, and let Him lead you toward healing.

Confess to God how you've been concealing your sin or guilt towards a friend in your life. What have you not taken ownership of yet?

Ask God to give you the courage to confess to your friend and ask for forgiveness.

Spend some time genuinely praying over your friend. Let God soften your heart toward them through your prayers.

WHEN I'M FEELING STUCK IN MY SIN

Mac

Therefore, since we also have such a large cloud of witnesses surrounding us, let us lay aside every hindrance and the sin that so easily ensnares us. Let us run with endurance the race that lies before us, keeping our eyes on Jesus, the pioneer and perfecter of our faith. For the joy that lay before him, he endured the cross, despising the shame, and sat down at the right hand of the throne of God.

Hebrews 12:1-2

Maybe you've been feeling stuck lately—stuck in the sin that you've tried so hard to throw off and escape from.

Perhaps it's the constant gossip you always find yourself participating in. Maybe it's the sin that you slip into behind closed doors when nobody's watching. It could even be the thoughts of hatred you have about yourself, your body, or someone who hurt you deeply.

The tricky thing about sin is that it can feel so satisfying in the moment, but it leaves a whole host of consequences that we're left to sort through after. It's almost like dancing in quicksand—you don't even notice what's beneath you because it's so fun and great. That is until you find yourself slowly sinking deeper and deeper until you can no longer find a way to escape.

Oftentimes, when we are trapped in a sin cycle, we unknowingly take our eyes off Jesus. But the writer of Hebrews tells us that if we are to lay aside every hindrance and sin to run the race that lies before us, then we must keep our eyes locked on Jesus. We look to Jesus because He is our example, our inspiration, and our Savior. He sacrificially took on the weight and death of all of our sin and guilt so we don't have to.

In ancient Greek, "keeping our eyes on Jesus" implied the idea of not only looking toward Jesus, but simultaneously looking away from all other things.[1]

When I get stuck in sin, it's often because I'm trying to keep one eye on Jesus while also keeping one eye on the things of this world—my desires, my comfort, my wellbeing, my popularity, and so on. These things don't start out as sin, but without Jesus as my primary vision, they quickly lead me in that direction. Other times, I've been so obsessed with overcoming my sin that I've fixated on the sin rather than looking to Jesus for the strength to overcome it.

I cannot promise you that overcoming any sort of sin pattern will be easy, but I do know the only way you can do it is by locking your gaze on Jesus and only Jesus.

Search your heart with God and look for any sin pattern that you've been trying to manage on your own.

Get honest with Jesus about the things you've been looking to for identity, worth, and purpose other than Jesus.

Spend a few minutes with Jesus and ask Him to help you fix your eyes on Him.

1. David Guzik, "Hebrews 12," *Enduring Word*, August 24, 2018, https://enduringword.com/bible-commentary/hebrews-12/.

WHEN I'M FEELING UNFORGIVABLE

Mac

_____

For we do not have a high priest who is unable to empathize with our weaknesses, but we have one who has been tempted in every way, just as we are—yet he did not sin. Let us then approach God's throne of grace with confidence, so that we may receive mercy and find grace to help us in our time of need.

Hebrews 4:15-16, NIV

Have you ever had a moment when you felt unforgivable? I most definitely have, and even though it was years ago, I still cringe thinking back upon it.

In my first year after college, I woke up one morning in a strange fluorescent room to a very kind nurse telling me that I was in the hospital. Although I had no memories of what had happened, I immediately knew why I was there.

The night before I had gone out with my friends for a "fun" evening in downtown Nashville. Although I had zero intentions of getting drunk, the perfect storm of not having much experience with alcohol, not eating much that day, and friends who were used to having a really good time, led to me drinking way too much and my body essentially shutting down.

I remember lying in that hospital bed feeling so much guilt, shame, embarrassment and fear mixed together in one. At the time, I worked in ministry, discipled other leaders, and was an example for hundreds of young girls. How could I do this? How was God ever going to forgive me? How could He use me again?

In the weeks following, I had to deal with some heavy consequences of my actions. I thought the worst part would be paying for the hospital bills and telling my parents and accountability partners, but the toughest part was wrestling with the constant feeling that I didn't deserve anyone's forgiveness or grace.

At first, I tried to hide from those feelings by attempting to somehow earn my way back into God's favor. Yet no matter what I tried, I couldn't shake that feeling of being not enough. One day, I stumbled upon Hebrews 4 in my Bible, and I knew it was God speaking to me. In that moment, He wanted me to stop running from Him, and instead, approach His throne with confidence so I could receive an outpouring of His grace.

For so long, I was always the girl who made the right decisions and never got in trouble. But there I was caught directly in my sin, and somehow that made God's love for me feel more real than it ever had before. For the first time in my life, I understood that God didn't send His Son to die on the cross for me because of how good I was, but because of how good He is.

Perhaps you've been believing that because of what you've done, you don't deserve His forgiveness. I challenge you to take the words of Hebrews seriously because God's shocking grace and mercy only get more powerful and beautiful when we find ourselves in desperate need of it.

Is there something from your past or your present that has left you feeling unforgivable? Get super honest with God about it!

Allow God to speak into your guilt. How do you walk forward in light of Him forgiving you?

Ask God to give you a new perspective and understanding of His grace today.

WHEN I'M FEELING LIKE I DON'T CARE

Mac

_____

I will give you a new heart and put a new spirit within you;
I will remove your heart of stone and give you a heart of flesh.
I will place my Spirit within you and cause you to follow my statutes
and carefully observe my ordinances.

Ezekiel 36:26-27

Sometimes, unprocessed feelings like guilt, hurt, anger, or sadness can lead us to shut off our hearts altogether. Rather than face those feelings head on, we'd rather escape to a fantasy land where attractive guys give out roses or people date in pods.

I went through a serious season of my life when I felt incredibly numb. Good and bad things would happen, and I wouldn't feel a thing. I would say or do things that I knew went against God's best for me, but I didn't seem to care. I stopped praying, reading my Bible, and even hanging with friends. Instead, I would binge Netflix, text cute boys for attention, and eat McDonald's McFlurries to at least give me a fleeting high.

My heart had grown numb because I did everything I could to avoid the unprocessed guilt, bitterness, and resentment I felt in my heart. Have you been there?

In this passage, we see God beginning to deliver His message of hope for the future of Israel through the prophet, Ezekiel. Although their hearts had strayed from His, God's heart would stop at nothing to pursue and chase them down. God was getting ready to do a new thing. He was sending a new King, and He was going to give them a new heart!

When I finally recognized my heart's condition in my own numbing season, I made the choice to run back to God. What I found is that even though I had quit on Him for a season, God had never quit on me. I decided to surrender to His heart transplant process. The next few months felt like God taking my heart, turning it upside down, and shaking it over and over again until every last embarrassing, ugly, sinful, and broken thing was in a pile at my feet. I had to pick up every piece and surrender it back to Him. While this process was extremely painful, it created the space for God to reawaken, realign, and recenter my heart on Him again.

If you've been feeling like you can't get yourself to care about anything, let alone God's best in your life, I challenge you to look for the ways that God has been continually pursuing you. Hand your numb, broken heart to Him and allow Him to replace it with a new one full of life and joy in Him. I can promise you that He's the best heart surgeon out there!

Spend some time reflecting on how God has been pursuing your heart all this time. Praise Him for that!

Meditate on Ezekiel 36:26-27. Spend some time confessing the habits in your life that perhaps have led to the hardening of your heart.

Ask God to begin His heart transplant process for you. Spend some time simply surrendering your heart before Him.

WHEN I'M FEELING UPSET ABOUT A DECISION I MADE

Mac

———

If we say, "We have no sin," we are deceiving ourselves, and the truth is not in us. If we confess our sins, he is faithful and righteous to forgive us our sins and to cleanse us from all unrighteousness.

1 John 1:8-9

Have you ever wanted to sweep a bad decision under the rug or act like it never even happened? Maybe it was the hurtful words you screamed at your friend in a fight, the website you look at when you were feeling lonely, or the choice you made last Friday night out with your friends.

Oftentimes, we like to assume that if we just ignore our sin, it will simply go away and eventually fade into the background. All we have to do is cover it up with enough good deeds or consecutive days of reading our Bible.

However, many of us have also experienced how unconfessed sin tends to fester and plant deep roots in our hearts preventing us from ever being able to overcome it. Sin begins to control us and leave us in chains to its power.

Scripture tells us that when we run from our sin, ignore it, dismiss it, diminish it, or sweep it under the rug, we're only deceiving ourselves. However, if we simply confess it, we are given an invitation into God's grace-filled forgiveness and beautiful transformation process.

Your path to freedom from sin, poor decisions, or regret doesn't come with your own ability to "be good" and refrain from making that decision again. Your freedom comes when you confess, accept God's forgiveness, and step into a new future with Him.

Perhaps you've been trying to manage your sin or any poor decisions on your own. I challenge you to run to Jesus, search every narrow passageway of your heart, confess every last thing before Him, accept that undeserved forgiveness, and let Him cleanse you of all the ways you've fallen short.

When you have received His forgiveness, you can walk in total freedom. And freedom isn't never messing up. It's not being so good that you don't even need God's grace. Freedom isn't striving to be better. It's not an escape from sin, temptation, pain, or guilt. Freedom isn't about what we do or don't do for Jesus. Freedom is all about what He did for us on that cross.

Would you let confession lead you into newfound freedom with Him?

Ask God to thoroughly search your heart. Is there any unconfessed sin that you need to confess?

Reflect on 1 John 1:8-9. Ask God for His forgiveness in your sins and to cleanse you of any unrighteousness.

Pray that God would give you a clear understanding of what freedom from your sin could be like with Him.

SECTION 8

JOY

We've made it to our final feeling, and this is one that I'm sure we've all been excited about! We're going to be diving into true joy— a joy that's not manufactured in Hallmark moments, the fun college party scenes you see in movies, or the happily ever afters you read about in every romance novel when the two lovebirds finally end up together. This feeling can only be found in Jesus!

Have you ever thought about the difference between happiness and joy? Happiness is those moments when everything seems to go right, all is well in the world, and the credit scenes roll with the happy music. But because we live in the real world, we know that life goes on after the movie ends and things often start to get difficult again. Your finances get tight, you don't get the job you wanted, the trip gets canceled, they stop loving you back, and your happiness is gone just like that. Happiness is an emotional roller coaster because it's attached to circumstances that are ever changing.

Joy is much different. It's something that we have to choose every day despite our circumstances. It's the willingness to embrace the good and the bad days, knowing that there is joy that can still be found.

It's funny, actually really scary, how easily we can start suppressing our feelings, running away from them, and pretending we're fine. You've probably noticed that all throughout these devotionals. You're like, "What? I didn't even know I was feeling this way," or "How did this even happen to me and I didn't feel it?"

Maybe it's because you've been missing true joy? You've been avoiding your feelings through cheap pleasures and quick fixes, jumping to that happy ending rather than being willing to feel it all, even when it's tough.

No matter what emotions we feel, joy can always be found. It's found when we raise our hands in worship, even when it feels hard. It's found when we get on our knees to pray in our bedroom, even when we feel defeated. It's found when we get up and run to the altar, even when

we feel stuck in our sin. It's found when we open our mouths and speak to Jesus, even when He feels far away.

Because joy is found when we are in relationship with the Author, the Creator, and the King of all joy!

As you dive into this last week, I pray that you will choose joy regardless of what you might be feeling. Our God is offering you an invitation to a joy that will satisfy you long past any fleeting moments of happiness.

WHEN I'M FEELING LIKE IT'S HARD TO FIND JOY

Kenz

*As a deer longs for flowing streams, so I long for you, God.
I thirst for God, the living God. When can I come and appear
before God? My tears have been my food day and night, while all day
long people say to me, "Where is your God?" I remember this as I pour
out my heart: how I walked with many, leading the festive procession to
the house of God, with joyful and thankful shouts.*

Psalm 42:1-4

How often do you go to the Lord in prayer and the first few words out of your mouth are, "Dear Jesus, thank you for _____"?

That's how I begin almost every single prayer. And while I do wholeheartedly believe in the importance of showing God my gratitude, that intro to my prayers has become so routine to me that it feels practically meaningless at this point.

How's that for vulnerable honesty?

But as I read these verses in Psalm 42, I was compelled to get honest about my own prayer life. Because while the writer of these verses used some raw and real words to express to God how they were feeling, I am often still stuck using the same exact phrases and words to talk to God.

To be completely honest with you (again), some mornings I wake up just plain grumpy. Other times, I feel completely defeated and ready to give up. Sometimes, I'm overwhelmed by my to-do list and lazily sit there with zero excitement to talk to God. Many days, all I really want to do is cry! And in those moments, rather than bringing my raw honesty to God through prayer, I find myself sitting there perfectly postured, coffee in hand, journal on my lap with my heart in the other room. Anyone else relate?

But God wants you to come Him with all of your feelings and emotions. Like any other best friend, you shouldn't hide the way you feel from Him. He wants to be in it with you and show you what He can offer you outside of your circumstances.

So if you're having a bad day or bad year, get honest with Him. He is waiting to meet you with love, truth, and you guessed it—joy!

Spend some time sitting with the Lord and opening up about the things that have been hard for you in this season.

Go to Psalm 42 in your Bible and underline any truths you see about the love and joy He is offering you despite how you feel.

As you go about your day, even if it's a hard one, look for moments of joy around you and trust in the Lord's love for you.

WHEN I'M FEELING THANKFUL

Kenz

Hallelujah! Praise God in his sanctuary. Praise him in his mighty expanse. Praise him for his powerful acts; praise him for his abundant greatness. Praise him with the blast of a ram's horn; praise him with harp and lyre. Praise him with tambourine and dance; praise him with strings and flute. Praise him with resounding cymbals; praise him with clashing cymbals. Let everything that breathes praise the LORD. Hallelujah!

Psalm 150:1-6

People often say that it's easier to be consistent with their time with Jesus and stay more connected to Him when life has been tough, rather than when things are going smoothly. It's almost like the harder life is, the more it compels us to be with Him. So the question is, how can we stay connected to Him when life feels good and even blissful?

I think we find the answer in Psalm 150.

This last chapter of Psalms is a passionate plead for all of creation, including you and I, to give God all of our praise.

There are days when it definitely feels easier to give God all of our praise, but this should be our everyday posture to the Lord. Whether on our worst days or our very best days, we can lift our hands in worship, sing these words out loud, and give God praise for what He is doing. On the days when things feel like we have a reason to sing praise to God, we should do so without an agenda. We shouldn't be looking for something or expecting anything in return. We can simply and joyfully praise Him for being who He is and His loving-kindness toward us.

There is always so much to be grateful for, so let praise be your default. Let every good thing happening in your life be another reason to worship your heavenly Father, because it keeps you in connection with Him—the giver of all good things (James 1:17).

Like this Psalm, I encourage you to spend some time today listing all the things you are thankful for. Write it down in the notes section in the back of this devotional, so you will always have a personal reminder of His greatness available to you!

Create a list or maybe even try writing a little poem or song about all the things you are grateful for.

Go somewhere where you can turn on some worship music and spend some time praising Him through song.

Invite the Lord into your joyful moments today, and ask Him to consistently remind you of His goodness.

WHEN I'M FEELING BEAUTIFUL

Kenz

But the Lord said to Samuel, "Do not look at his appearance or his stature because I have rejected him. Humans do not see what the Lord sees, for humans see what is visible, but the Lord sees the heart."

1 Samuel 16:7

The Lord thinks you are beautiful—that is for sure! The way He made you is perfect and He's so proud of it. From the curves on your body, the hairs on your head, and the freckles on your face. Nothing about you was a mistake. There's nothing He would do differently. You are His treasured creation.

But beyond your external beauty, God's even more proud of your internal beauty. He cares most about what's going on in your heart. He sees what's going on inside of you, the passing thoughts, small conversations, and the way you treat others that most people might overlook.

In 1 Samuel 16:7, the Lord emphasizes to Samuel what He is looking for in a king. Most people thought a king would need to be someone big and strong to intimidate the enemy and someone confident enough to defeat any giant.

As humans, we are often blinded by good looks and impressive resumes. It's so easy for us to overlook good character and get fixated on outward appearances. We spend hours on end getting ready in the morning, spend so much money shopping, and revolve our entire lives around building an impressive career. But all the while, the Lord just looks at what's going on inside. He wants to use anyone who's simply sold out for Him and bearing the fruit of it throughout their personal life.

Joy truly is found when we let go of our "impress mode" and simply live out Christlikeness in everything we do. When you build your life centered on Him and His Word, you can both rejoice in the way He created you and confidently walk in the way He has called you.

Spend some time jotting down the parts of your character that you might not always acknowledge, but are so beautiful to the Lord.

Meditate on the heart of God and how He sees beauty in you.

Ask the Lord to help you see people around you, then confidently carry that new perspective of beauty into your everyday life.

WHEN I'M FEELING SEEN IN MY MESS

Kenz

―――

The angel of the LORD said to her, "You have conceived and will have a son. You will name him Ishmael, for the LORD has heard your cry of affliction. This man will be like a wild donkey. His hand will be against everyone, and everyone's hand will be against him; he will settle near all his relatives." So she named the LORD who spoke to her: "You are El-roi," for she said, "In this place, have I actually seen the one who sees me?"

Genesis 16:11-13

Have you been waiting for a mountain top moment to experience joy? You've unknowingly convinced yourself that you cannot experience the fullness of joy because of how your life looks right now. But what I learn from this piece of Scripture is that some of the most authentic joy can be found in life's toughest moments. Because it's often right there in the middle of the mess of life that we realize God sees us and He is oh so good.

Here in Genesis 16, we meet a woman named Hagar. I'd recommend reading the full chapter to truly discover how much of a mess Hagar has found herself in. To quickly sum up her life troubles for you, she was a slave of Abram and Sarai who struggled having kids. Sarai finally suggested that Abram sleep with Hagar in hopes that she could build a family through her. Well the deed was done, and Hagar became pregnant. That led to Sarai's bitterness, leaving a pregnant Hagar almost no choice but to run away or else continue to endure Sarai's mistreatment.

In Genesis 16:7, it says "The angel of the LORD found her by a spring in the wilderness." From a human perspective, it doesn't seem rational that out of all the things He could be doing, God would choose to show up before a pregnant servant in the middle of the wilderness and promise her blessings. But that's exactly what He did. God told her to go back to Sarai, even though it might be hard, and the Lord would honor her obedience and multiply her offspring.

In the middle of Hagar's mess and in what was probably her lowest moment, the Lord sought her out. I believe Hagar's response in naming God as the One who sees—*El-roi*—was an act of worship. Her circumstances hadn't changed, but Hagar had encountered the God who saw her mess and still sought her out.

That is joy. It's not circumstantial or a temporary feeling of happiness. It's realizing that in the middle of our mess, we can always encounter our heavenly Father. I cannot tell you how many times my circumstances have been absolutely horrendous but a moment with Jesus in the midst of it everything changed. There's truly no better feeling than knowing your God sees, understands, and has plans to restore and redeem what has been lost as you walk step by step with Him.

You don't have to hold out for joy any longer. Believe that your Father sees you here in the middle of whatever you're facing, and that you can encounter all of His goodness no matter what mess you find yourself in.

Identify areas where you've been holding out to experience joy.

Imagine yourself in Hagar's position and finally feeling seen by the Lord. How does her story help you understand authentic joy? Respond in worship.

Invite the Lord into your current situation and ask Him to restore your joy.

WHEN I'M FEELING LIKE I NEED A LITTLE EXTRA HOPE

Kenz

Therefore, since we have been justified by faith, we have peace with God through our Lord Jesus Christ. We have also obtained access through him by faith into this grace in which we stand, and we boast in the hope of the glory of God. And not only that, but we also boast in our afflictions, because we know that affliction produces endurance, endurance produces proven character, and proven character produces hope. This hope will not disappoint us, because God's love has been poured out in our hearts through the Holy Spirit who was given to us.

Romans 5:1-5

As you probably know by now, life isn't always going to be easy. There are going to be days when you are sad, moments when you are straight up angry, situations that are extremely hurtful, and changes that are really lonely. But Romans 5 says that we should "boast in our afflictions" because we know what it produces: endurance, character, and hope.

Did you know that you have access to that hope today? Scripture reveals that this is not a flippant, wishful kind of hope. It's not a hope that good times on earth are heading our way or that all of our problems will disappear with a boyfriend, job offer, or better friend group.

Our hope is our salvation. If you are a follower of Jesus, your hope is secure in Jesus because of what He did on the cross. That means that no matter what our circumstances may feel like or look like, Jesus's love and the work of the Holy Spirit remains steadfast. And if everything on earth fails us, we still have the hope of eternity with Him.

So while our life on earth may never look like we "hope" it will, we are guaranteed that heaven will be everything we want and more because Jesus will be there. He is our hope. And if we have Jesus, we have all that we need.

Therefore, on the days when you just don't feel like getting up and life feels super heavy, remember this: if you have a relationship with Jesus, you have hope. It's never going away, it cannot be taken from you, and it will never change.

Invite the Lord into your sorrows and where you've been tempted to give up hope.

Spend some time reading all of Romans 5 and reflect on how your definition of hope has been redefined.

Ask the Lord to fill your heart with hope and to restore your life with joy.

Notes

FOR WHEN I'M IN MY FEELS

Notes

Notes

FOR WHEN I'M IN MY FEELS

Notes

FOR WHEN I'M IN MY FEELS

WANT TO GO DEEPER IN YOUR STUDY OF FEELINGS IN GOD'S WORD?

BIBLE STUDY FOR COLLEGE WOMEN

MAC BRIDGES / KENZ DURHAM

IN MY FEELS

HOW TO FEEL GOD WHEN I'M NOT FEELING IT

FOR WHEN I'M IN MY FEELS